40

Restorative Justice and Victim-Offender Mediation

40 Cases

Restorative Justice and Victim-Offender Mediation

Edited by Paul Crosland and Marian Liebmann

 Mediation UK

Published by Mediation UK
Alexander House
Telephone Avenue
Bristol
BS1 4BS
0117 904 6661
enquiry@mediationuk.org.uk
www.mediationuk.org.uk
Registered Charity no. 1019275

First published October 2003

ISBN 1-872756-87-5

Designed and artworked by Puffin Design 01453 753123

Printed by TL Visuals Limited, Yate, Bristol 01454 319555

Introduction

The aim of the book

How can we connect our vision of Restorative Justice with the real ways in which victims, offenders and communities seek to address the aftermath of a crime?

Case studies are a valuable tool in enabling us to build bridges between theories and practice. They also widen our imagination to see more of the actual range of issues, feelings, needs and strategies that either do or don't help people and communities meet their individual and collective needs.

This book provides a diverse range of first hand accounts from mediators and facilitators offering some means of communication between victims and offenders. Through the authentic voices of practitioners, the cases unfold to reveal how communication was facilitated and the outcomes that followed.

This publication aims to provide practitioners, policy makers and interested professionals with:

- Opportunities to compare practice
- An examination of the appropriateness of offering access to Restorative Justice
- An understanding of the subtleties of facilitated victim-offender communication
- An opportunity to see beyond our own preconceptions of victims and offenders
- Clarity and inspiration

A just representation of Restorative Justice

One definition of Restorative Justice is:

Restorative Justice seeks to balance the concerns of the victim and the community with the need to reintegrate the offender into society. It seeks to assist the recovery of the victim and enable all parties with a stake in the justice process to participate fruitfully in it.

(Restorative Justice Consortium)

If you want to read about other definitions of Restorative Justice, this book includes a brief bibliography. What all the definitions have in common is that they include victims, offenders and the community, and aim to put right the harm done by crime.

Restorative Justice is often misrepresented as only a diversionary process in Criminal Justice rather than as an approach to be applied across all stages of criminal justice. Although some restorative work leads to diversion from other criminal justice processes, many case stories in this book show how much restorative work there is still to do after sentencing.

Whilst some work is more restorative in process and outcomes than other work, no such classification system is being used in this book to define what is and isn't being respectfully restored to victim, offender and community. The approach of this book is to simply offer accounts of what is being done in the name of restorative justice and victim-offender mediation. So here are 40 accounts of what Restorative Justice does. No cases that have been sent in to be published have been excluded and the editing pen has only been lightly used so that the practitioner voice is clear. To those 28 practitioners who contributed cases, thanks are extended in sharing their experience for others to learn from.

From Restorative Justice practice-speak to a common language

Much restorative work is undertaken under different titles which emphasise the differences at the expense of highlighting the similarities. So a catch-all phrase 'restorative meetings' is sometimes useful to cover the differently structured face-to-face meetings: victim-offender mediation, restorative conferencing, family group meetings/conferences and the new hybrid process used in Referral Orders/Youth Offender Panels. In addition to 'restorative meetings' there is the crucial indirect mediation work (sometimes called 'shuttle mediation') that is often a vital process before, after or totally independent of any meeting. And what do we call the people who do both 'indirect mediation' and 'restorative conferencing'? Let's settle for 'mediator/facilitator'.

As Restorative Justice has become a more popular phrase its use has been adopted in settings which do not have the key distinguishing features of the law having identified an offender and a victim. Whilst 'restorative approaches' might better describe some work where there is no legally defined offender and victim, this book has been broad enough to include some accounts of behaviour in schools which technically could have been treated as crimes but were instead treated via restorative approaches. That there was a harm to be addressed was acknowledged by the participants; that there was a crime was not acknowledged. Restorative approaches can often resolve these 'grey area' situations more constructively than purely legal approaches.

Rather than elaborating on the community debates about the definition of and response to crime and what restorative processes have to offer to the development of these dialogues, the focus of this book is on the individuals who want communication which goes beyond the labels put on them of 'victim' and 'offender'.

Restorative Justice without the engagement of victim or offender

All 40 cases involve communication between 'victim' (or 'secondary victim') and 'offender'. Another book would be needed to cover all the restorative work that goes on where the opportunity for communication has been lost or the offender not been caught. The following list is an indication of restorative communication which has been undertaken but which lies outside this book of mainstream UK restorative meetings and shuttle mediations:

- Victim's groups inputting project ideas (and receiving feedback) in relation to community reparation schemes
- Sentencing circles (a Canadian model)
- Circles of Support and Accountability (mostly undertaken in relation to release plans for sex offenders)
- Victim–Offender Groups (e.g. facilitated between known burglars and the victims of unknown burglars)
- Offender meeting a 'surrogate victim'
- Victim meeting a 'surrogate offender'
- Restorative Justice Practitioner adopting the persona of a 'compassionate perpetrator' talking to the actual victim (where involvement of the perpetrator or compassion from the perpetrator has not been forthcoming)
- Restorative Justice Practitioner talking to the offender in the persona of a victim expressing their needs and understanding (where involvement of the victim has not been forthcoming)

There are many inadequately explored processes which might empower

---

victims', offenders' and communities' search for understanding and (re-)connection after a crime. The search is held back by limited opportunities to explore feelings, needs and requests in the context of criminal justice. The possibilities are inevitably limited by our imagination, experience and collective learning of what is possible and what is 'appropriate'.

Which criminal cases are appropriate for restorative work?

The idea of producing this collection of case-studies was sparked by the use of the word 'appropriate' in a 2001 European Council Decision on the standing of victims in criminal proceedings. The wording of the European Council Decision was that each member state should 'promote mediation in criminal cases for offences which it considers appropriate for this sort of measure'. If appropriateness is to be decided based on a legalistic offence category and not on the needs of victims, offenders and communities, then the application of restorative principles in the criminal justice system will be very limited.

That is the question that this book leaves the reader with. Was the appropriate work undertaken in each of the case studies and how can we ensure the availability of appropriate restorative work?

'Mediatable offences include all crimes which involve clearly identifiable victims and offenders. These offences include arson, assault, burglary, deception, car theft, theft from employer, robbery, kidnapping, violent assaults of all levels of seriousness, sexual assaults and domestic violence...It is important not to have preconceptions about 'suitable' cases, as it is victims' and offenders' perceptions which determine suitability, not mediators'.

(Wynne, J., p136 in Mediation in Context, Liebmann, M., 2000)

Some practice issues raised in this book

The bullet points labelled 'Reflections' at the end of most of the case studies highlight some practice issues. As a pre-cursor to these points here is a brief list of 'Key features of effective restorative practice':
- Facilitators impartial
- Facilitators appropriately trained
- Perpetrator accepts responsibility
- Realistic and informed choice

- No pressure on victims
- Thorough preparation for all participants
- Acknowledgement that views of all are important
- All parties involved
- Solutions agreed by all parties
- Perpetrators encouraged to be accountable for own actions
- Restorative meeting before reparation

(Youth Justice Board Good Practice Guidelines (Feb 2001))

This book provides practical examples of benefits from mediated/facilitated victim-offender communication.

Victims have the opportunity to:
- Learn about the offender and put a face to the crime
- Ask questions of the offender
- Express their feelings and needs after the crime
- Receive an apology and/or appropriate reparation
- Educate offenders about the effects of their offences
- Sort out any existing conflict
- Be part of the criminal justice process
- Put the crime behind them

Offenders have the opportunity to:
- Own the responsibility for their crime
- Find out the effect of their crime
- Apologise and/or offer appropriate reparation
- Reassess their future behaviour in the light of this knowledge

Courts have the opportunity to:
- Learn about victims' needs
- Aid reparative purposes in sentencing

Communities have the opportunity to
- Accept apologies and reparation from offenders
- Help reintegrate victims and offenders

The layout of the book

This book is arranged in order of which stage of the criminal justice process the restorative work was commenced (and in some cases, completed).

The stages into which the cases have been grouped are as follows:
1) Not prosecuted/Diversion
2) Reprimand/ Final Warning
3) Preparation of Pre-Sentence Report
4) Serving a community sentence
5) Serving a custodial sentence
6) Post custody (on licence)

Not all possible stages have been represented in these case studies; e.g. sentence being deferred for restorative intervention, or post sentence at request of victim or offender.

Some cases have been written in the third person and some in the first person. All cases have been anonymised.

The views of the contributors should not be interpreted as endorsed by Mediation UK.

Mediation UK has (since its inception in 1984) represented and promoted victim-offender mediation and the wider development of Restorative Justice.

Acknowledgements

Sincere thanks are extended to all contributors (listed below) without whom this publication would not be possible:

- Bracknell Forest Youth Offending Team
- Derbyshire Youth Offending Service
- East Sussex Youth Offending Team
- Face to Face, York
- Greater Manchester Victim Support
- Greater Manchester Youth Justice Trust
- Hawick Youth Offending Service
- Leeds Victim Offender Unit
- Leicestershire Youth Offending Service
- Maidstone Mediation
- Mediation Buckinghamshire
- Medway Youth Offending Team
- MILAN (Mediation in Lancashire)
- North Tyneside Youth Offending Team
- North Yorkshire Youth Offending Team
- Nottingham City Youth Offending Team
- Oxfordshire Youth Offending Team
- REMEDI -Doncaster
- REMEDI -Sheffield
- Thames Valley Police
- The Children's Society
- Tower Hamlets Mediation Service
- West Mercia Police
- West Midlands Probation Service
- Wrexham Youth Offending Service

Mediation UK also acknowledges the invaluable work of Richard Desmond, Volunteer Research Assistant. Thanks are also due to members of the Mediation UK Mediation and Reparation Committee in guiding this publication and to the Mediation UK staff team in giving their comments, suggestions and time in the development of this project.

List of cases

Section 1 **Not prosecuted/diversion** 1

CASE 1 **Shuttle mediation when no charges have been brought** 2

A 15 year old boy punched a female friend, causing tension between the two families, and one party making threatening phone calls. A shuttle mediation resolved the issues.

Section 2 **Reprimand/final warning** 7

CASE 2 **Theft of handbag and mobile phone from teacher.** 8

Three 14 year old boys took a handbag and mobile phone off a teacher's desk. The School set up a meeting with the boys and their parents.

CASE 3 **Theft: young mother took ring from jewellers** 9

An opportunistic theft led to a meeting and police caution.

CASE 4 **Assault: retaliation is an assault with wide effects in school** 10

A 16 year old was reprimanded for assault.
When he re-appeared in school, he was assaulted by the victim.
The Mediation Service was called in.

CASE 5 **Theft from sheltered housing** 13

A teenage boy took keys from sheltered housing and stole money.

CASE 6 **Damage to school classroom** 16

Four 15 year old boys broke into school buildings and caused considerable damage. A restorative Justice Conference took place at the scene of the damage.

CASE 7 **Stabbing: a bullied boy snapped, resulting in wounding** 20

A 14 year old male stabbed another boy in the back with scissors after enduring bullying.

CASE 8 **Burglary of a factory** 24

A group of boys broke into factory, damaged machines and lit a series of small fires. The factory owner accepted the apology and offered one of the boys a job if he stayed out of trouble.

CASE 9 **Assault following longstanding tensions** 27

A girl assaulted another girl with a vodka bottle. Both girls saw themselves as the victims.

CASE 10 **Criminal damage to a church** 29

Three boys (aged16 –17) broke church windows and wrote offensive words around the church door. Reparation was carried out.

Section 3 **Preparation of pre-sentence report** 33

CASE 11 **Disorder offence: offender was a victim; police officer becomes victim; how is humanity regained?** 34

Woman in her forties was drunk and disorderly in police station and needed to explain how much despair she felt after her last encounter with the Criminal Justice System

CASE 12 **Robbery of an elderly woman** 38

Two boys (aged 14 and 15) robbed an elderly woman's handbag and knocked her over causing shock, distress and injury.

CASE 13 **Street robbery at knifepoint** 43

A 15 year old boy was robbed by 2 boys who attended the same school. Following a meeting, a detailed agreement was made.

Section 4 **Serving a community sentence** 47

CASE 14 **Theft from store** 48

A boy stole a computer game from a large store. Following a meeting, the Store Manager offered the offender a work experience placement.

CASE 15 **Indecent assault on sisters' best friend** 51

The Family Group Meetings Project explored the possibility of a face-to-face meeting between victim and offender.

CASE 16 **Aggravated taking without owners' consent - an angry victim** 58

A 16 year old boy stole a camper-van and crashed it. The angry victim was dismissive about mediation but eventually agreed to meet the offender.

CASE 17 **Criminal damage to a vehicle** 61

A 17 year old jumped along the roofs of vehicles when drunk, causing £2,800 of damage to an Alpha Romeo.

CASE 18 **Public order offence following a final warning for a similar incident with the same victim** 64

A 16 year old male was involved in an incident with a 16 year old boy who was known to him in a local park. The offender had already received a Final Warning for an assault on the same victim.

CASE 19 **Assault on a peer** 69

A 12 year old boy assaulted a fellow pupil after a history of classroom bullying.

CASE 20 **Assault with actual bodily harm** 71

A 15 year old girl accused a fellow school pupil of spreading rumours and then assaulted her causing actual bodily harm.

CASE 21 **Burglary of a family with young children** 74

A 13 year old boy burgled a family home, causing fear and distress to two young children.

CASE 22 **Arson in a small community** 76

Two 15 year old boys set fire to a primary school, burning the building to the ground.

CASE 23 **Indecent assault involving young people with learning difficulties** 80

A 13 year old boy indecently assaulted a 16 year old girl. Both the victim and offender had learning difficulties.

CASE 24 **Attempted robbery of an elderly shopkeeper** 83

Two 15 year old boys attempted to rob a local corner shop, threatening and frightening the elderly shopkeeper.

CASE 25 **Endangering persons using railways: a sack of manure** **86**

*Three teenage boys hung a sack of manure from a bridge.
When the train hit it, it obstructed the drivers vision and caused
distress to passengers.*

CASE 26 **Criminal damage: burnt bridges?** **88**

*A 15 year old boy sawed pieces of wood off a bridge and built a
fire which caused £2,500 worth of damage.*

CASE 27 **Assault on a former friend** **91**

*A 15 year old boy assaulted a former friend after being excluded
from school.*

CASE 28 **Assault with actual bodily harm: a victim living in fear** **94**

*A 15 year old boy assaulted a 17 year old boy, causing Actual
Bodily Harm. The victim was terrified of what would happen if
he saw the offender locally.*

CASE 29 **Criminal damage to a community centre** **96**

*A 15 year old boy smashed the windows of a Community
Centre whilst under the influence of alcohol.*

CASE 30 **Intent to supply drugs and burglary: a father and son mediation** **100**

*A mediation was set up for a father and son following the son's
criminal behaviour.*

CASE 31 **Criminal damage after a row with girlfriend** **103**

*A young man smashed an office window causing fear and
distress to the office workers inside.*

CASE 32 **Assault on a police officer by young woman under
the influence of alcohol** **105**

*A police officer was assaulted by a 17 year old whilst trying to
dress her in the cell as she was under the influence of alcohol.*

Section 5 **Serving a custodial sentence** 109

CASE 33 **Arson – seeing the emotional consequences of a burnt-out home 110**

14 year old boy set fire to some paper which was thrown by another boy and started a major house fire.

CASE 34 **Manslaughter- who is communicating with who?** **118**

A 17 year old was convicted of the manslaughter of his friend. Three generations of 'secondary' victims were apparent.

CASE 35 **Street robbery in a small community** **123**

A 17 year old was convicted of the manslaughter of his friend. Three generations of 'secondary' victims were apparent.

CASE 36 **Theft from a valued drug support worker** **126**

A client stole her key workers purse and misused her credit card.

CASE 37 **Burglary with high risk of re-offending** **128**

A prolific offender burgled a young mother's house. The victim and offender met for mediation in prison.

CASE 38 **Indecent assault on a young girl** **131**

A 15 year old boy indecently assaulted a young girl and physically assaulted her friend. The victim requested a meeting with the offender.

Section 6 **Post custody (on licence)** 137

CASE 39 **Rape: communication between brother and sister** **138**

An 18 year old raped his 13 year old sister. The victim and her mother sought communication with the offender.

CASE 40 **Robbery of an elderly woman** **143**

A 17 year old boy robbed an elderly woman causing serious injuries. The victim and offender later took part in a film about restorative justice.

Section 1

Not prosecuted/diversion

Case 1   Shuttle mediation when no charges have been brought

A 15 year old boy punched a female friend, causing tension between the two families, and one party making threatening phone calls. A shuttle mediation resolved the issues.

Background

Simon was a 15 year old with grown up siblings. He lived with his mother and father on a low-rise estate in a central but hard-to-get-to part of an inner city. Next-door-but-one lived his relative Zoë. Despite some past tension Simon was very close to Zoë and her family.

The Conflict

One Bonfire Night, Simon punched Zoë in the face because she taunted him, giving her a serious cut needing hospital treatment. No charges were made, but the incident ignited past tensions. Families, their neighbours and the teenagers' friends became involved. In the following months Simon and his mother complained of name-calling, insulting graffiti and rumours, shouting and 'dirty looks'. Zoë and her family made counter-allegations including drug use.

The Council Housing Office encouraged Simon and his mother to record incidents. The police were often called. Simon got into fights with Zoë's younger brothers and male friends and his nose was broken. No charges were brought, but the police began to investigate threatening telephone calls and text messages sent to Simon. Zoë and Simon effectively dropped out of their school. Zoë spent much time with relatives elsewhere, causing more rumours.

The police eventually put Simon in contact with the Victim Support

Restorative Justice Worker who handled victim contact in Youth Offending Team (Yot) cases. With great difficulty, she persuaded the Council's Anti-Social Behaviour Unit to refer the case to the local independent Mediation Service, which provided victim-offender mediation to the Yot, but had received very few referrals. It was now two years since Simon hit Zoë, but as the police (unknown to her) had identified Zoë and her friends as the threatening callers, it seemed likely that unless things improved the case would soon come to the Yot anyway.

The Mediation

The paid Victim Offender Mediation Co-ordinator and a Volunteer Mediator met with Simon and then visited Zoë's family as a whole. Simon was scared and regretted punching Zoë, but was caught up in incident recording and investigations, driven by his protective mother. Zoë, her father and her siblings were defiant. Both sides accused the other of aggravating the situation to get re-housed, but the Council had made it plain that Anti-Social Behaviour Contracts and eviction were more likely. Zoë's mother was very conscious of this.

Mediators arranged a meeting between Simon and Zoë within five weeks, with their mothers present as silent supporters. But on two occasions Simon's mother cancelled at the last moment, partly because of ongoing incidents, but seemingly also because of anxiety that the past would come up.

Zoë's mother and Simon were keen, but it seemed hopeless. Mediators therefore put the responsibility back on to the parties, allowed a natural break for Christmas, and did some telephone diplomacy. They then offered to shuttle between Simon and Zoë, with the Victim Support Restorative Justice worker accompanying Simon instead of his mother.

On the day, bad timing meant that Zoë and Pam (her supporter) had to walk past Simon to enter the mediation office and needed much reassurance. Mediators then spent four-and-a-half hours shuttling between the parties' in separate rooms.

Neither teenager wanted an ongoing relationship, but with the help of Zoë's mother and the Victim Support Worker they were able to generate a plan for ending interference from family and friends and managing unavoidable future contact.

The Result

The agreement was typed up and shuttled back and forth for signing. Some minor parts were vague, but both parties were too tired to continue and mediators felt that to set rules for future communication too strictly might prevent positive interaction once the immediate tension had calmed down. Simon and Zoë both asked if they could return if need be, and seemed to treat the document very seriously. This was eleven weeks after the referral.

Six months later the situation was still calm. Simon's mother was so pleased that she sent chocolates to the Victim Support worker. The Anti-Social Behaviour Officer involved has since expressed interest in using mediation in similar cases. National TV later interviewed young victims in the area, including Simon. He attended the premiere at a local film festival, and it has been shown in schools. However, possible charges over death threats may still cause the conflict to resurface.

Six months later the situation was still calm. Simon's mother was so pleased that she sent chocolates to the Victim Support worker.

Reflections

- The stage of the legal process at which this work took place was under investigation, but no arrest
- Victim-Offender Mediation Shuttle in same building
- The whole case took 11 weeks
- The use of mediation with Anti-Social Behaviour was effective
- The strong contrast between previous crisis and subsequent lack of incidents was striking. Request by the parties to come back to mediation if needs be was positive. Positive feedback from Simon and his mother.
- Issues assisting success: the mediators placed responsibility back on to parties. Both parties were aware of eviction risk. The offer of shuttle mediation in the same building was the breakthrough.
- Time/money savings: the paid mediator spent 19 hours in total, the volunteer mediator spent 13 hours. The alternative would have involved the police, council, Victim Support, health service, court and Youth

Offending Team, and the time and money involved in Anti-Social Behaviour Contracts, evictions and prosecutions.

- It was very difficult to persuade the Anti Social Behaviour Officer to refer the case to mediation. This case could have been referred to the Mediation Service under an existing contract with the Council Housing Unit much earlier in the dispute.
- This case shows how a crime can be based in a community conflict, which needs to be sorted out to prevent re-offending.

Section 2
Reprimand/final warning

Case 2   Theft of Handbag and Mobile Phone from Teacher

Three 14 year old boys took a handbag
and mobile phone off a teacher's desk.
The School set up a meeting with the boys
and their parents.

Three 14 year old boys had been instructed to collect a set of school books from the staff common room at their school. When there was no answer at the door they let themselves in, collected the books, but also took a handbag and mobile phone off a teacher's desk. Immediately under suspicion when the items were missed, the boys were confronted by the Deputy Head and owned up. They were suspended for 3 days and the police were called in.

The boys were asked to attend a meeting together with their mothers, their Year Head and the Deputy Head. A police Schools and Youth Liaison Officer, who visited the school regularly and worked closely with school staff to combat crime, anti-social behaviour and bullying, chaired the meeting. He asked the boys to describe what had happened and how they felt about it. The Deputy Head then recounted how the crime victim, a young female teacher known for her calm, rational approach to life, had nevertheless been deeply affected by the incident, to the extent that she did not feel able to attend the meeting. Their Year Head was massively disappointed that the boys had made decisions which had a major impact on other people's lives, whilst their mothers were furious. 'We've been burgled twice,' one of them said, 'he knows what it's like to have his stuff taken and we don't like it.'

> *"We all make mistakes, but there are now some bridges that need to be rebuilt around trust and honesty."*

Formal Police Reprimands were issued to the boys, and the meeting ended with them agreeing to write letters of apology to the Teacher.

'We all make mistakes,' said their Year Head, 'but there are now some bridges that need to be rebuilt around trust and honesty.'

Case 3   Theft: Young mother took ring from jewellers

An opportunistic theft led to a meeting and police caution.

Lisa, a young mother, went shopping with her children. She went into a jeweller's shop to buy a necklace. Whilst the Shop Assistant was running her credit card through the till, Lisa noticed a gold ring on the counter. Quietly she pocketed it. Later another customer returned to the shop to collect the ring, her own, having forgotten to put it back on after trying a new one. Unable to find it, she and the Shop Assistant put two and two together, so they called the Police to report a possible theft and to pass on Lisa's details from the credit card counterfoil.

In due course Lisa received a visit from a Police Officer, who spied the ring on her finger and arrested her. Interviewed at the local police station, she recounted what had happened. 'As soon as I got out I knew I'd done wrong. It was just so stupid. When the police came round I knew what they were there for – I knew it was just a matter of time. The first thing I thought of was my kids – they still don't know what I've done. Everything I taught them...I'm just a sham.'

Lisa handed over a letter of apology she had written, and was asked to come back to the police station the following week. 'We're not here to say you're a bad person, you've just made a mistake and this would help you put closure to it,' the officer said.

Lisa returned as requested, and met with a Store Manager representing the shopping centre where the theft had occurred. She heard from the Manager what a huge problem shoplifting was in the city, and told him how remorseful and ashamed she was for what she had done.

"I don't think she'll ever re-offend," the officer noted later.

Finally she met the Police Officer again to receive an official caution. 'I don't think she'll ever re-offend,' the officer noted later.

Case 4   Assault: retaliation is an assault with wide effects in school

A 16 year old was reprimanded for assault.
When he re-appeared in school, he was assaulted
by the victim. The Mediation Service was called in.

The background

Both boys were pupils at a high school and had both had a secondment to a building college where they were learning building skills and where the offence occurred.

Whilst there had been minor antagonism before there was no clear definition of what the flash-point was to cause Colin to hit Gareth with a hammer. The police had liaised over the case and Colin had been reprimanded for his assault on Gareth. It had been Gareth's parents who had reported the assault to the police. Gareth had come home and had then been taken to casualty by his parents, suffering from a delayed concussion from a hammer blow.

The school had already developed links with outside agencies in order to assist when they experienced problems. A police outreach worker attached to a high school referred this case on to the mediation service under the terms of an existing partnership agreement. Once the case was referred to our mediation service, I went to see Gareth first and then Colin.

Both boys had a perception of being both victim and offender because what happened was a fracas at the building college. Colin had picked up a hammer and swiped Gareth without causing a visible injury. Colin had been suspended from school and when he returned to school, Gareth saw red and beat Colin up, kicking him repeatedly on the ground. Both boys became both victim and offender in the incidents, though only Colin had been formally reprimanded by the police.

When I visited Gareth he felt justified in retaliating because he felt that the presence of Colin in the school made him feel threatened. He just felt that justice hadn't been done as he hadn't been taken to court and prosecuted for it. So there was confusion in them both. Part of my work was in developing an understanding that being a victim led to being an offender and enabling the owning of that title victim and offender in those respective situations.

It was not just a two-way mediation; but a three way mediation, including the Head Teacher of the school. Mr Jefferies, Headmaster, had been brought into dialogue first of all to give me some background information and understanding on the respective exclusions of the two boys and secondly because I wanted to back track and ask was there some history between the two boys in the first instance, was there was anything that predated the first incident at the building college?

"Part of my work was in developing an understanding that being a victim led to being an offender and enabling the owning of that title victim and offender in those respective situations."

Mr Jefferies was very clear about what he wanted to come out of the mediation. He wanted the two boys to take on board the owning of their own offences and understanding of how their respective offences had affected each other as victims. He wanted some resolution so that this wasn't going to be an ongoing thing which would then spill back into the school when the two of them were back into the same environment. The fact that Mr Jefferies had given me background information was very productive for the mediation because it helped me understand why there was a discrepancy in the length of times they were both banned form school. One had been banned for less time than the other one and that was an issue for both the boys.

Gareth saw that he'd been banned for longer than Colin when in actual fact he was actually being excluded for the same number of days attendance at school. Holidays and two weeks work experience accounted for the longer period before Gareth was to be allowed back to school.

In the face-to-face meeting Mr Jefferies took very much a back seat role, he was present, the two boys were present, Colin had his mum there but Gareth chose not to have anyone else there, not seeing the need for it. I worked with a co-mediator, at the meeting. We stated clearly that Mr Jefferies was there to see what was going on and to use that to put on school record in relation to the two boys. Nonetheless, during the mediation Mr

Jefferies offered the flexibility to reduce Gareth's school-exclusion, allowing a negotiation between the two boys themselves. Mr Jefferies said to Colin "How do you feel now after hearing what's been said and discussed, if I allow Gareth back into the school? We've heard all the assurances that nothing was going to kick off any further." Mr Jefferies also wanted to take what he'd heard back to the school to a specific teacher who had witnessed the assault in the school and while she had not been involved in it, had been very shocked by it as a very aggressive act that had come out of nowhere. She needed re-assurance before she was able to accept the early return of the boys to school and was content with the headmaster's role in expressing her upset at the mediation and relaying an account back to her. There was a need for similar dialogue between Mr Jefferies and the staff that actually teach the boys.

During the mediation, Colin and Gareth came to see their assaults on each other as stones being thrown into a pond, that cause many ripples. Families, teachers and non-teaching staff were all affected.

Then Colin and Gareth looked at how they could have prevented their behaviour from escalating in the way it had, and what they would like to have done differently.

Mr Jefferies greatly valued the externally facilitated mediation process as a means of emphasising the seriousness of the concerns. From his perspective, the mediation enabled somebody else to take responsibility for the meeting whilst he expressed various concerns and enabled the engagement of the offenders in ways that wouldn't have happened if he had just given them a telling-off.

There were apologies on both sides and when involved with young people, if it has been a positive face-to-face and both are making resolutions towards making change, I offer them the option of shaking hands together. These two without hesitation shook hands with each other. I feel that personally, if two people make that connection that it cements their resolve not to continue the behaviour. Also it allowed the two boys to 'put it to bed'. The two boys are from an environment in their town that could have allowed the animosity to continue and build over months and years. On Colin's part there was an element of being the 'main man', of being seen as a 'wide boy'. They would have perpetuated this and it would have gone on in the school. It was an intervention that was witnessed by people who were relevant to them – allowing them formally to declare 'war was over'.

Reflections

- The success of the mediation process was of a mutual understanding and learning from it on all sides.
- The case was an example of the need for rules and exclusions to be fully explained and relevant others informed when someone is due to be back in their environment.
- The mediation by an external agency showed the parents that the school was dealing with the matter seriously.
- Mediation, either instead of going to court or after going to court, was the only way that these two boys were going to develop an awareness and understanding of each other and of their offences. The young person has something to gain from this, we're not just being retributive.
- For the boys the important thing was that both were given the forum to explain themselves and ask questions of each other in a non-threatening face-to-face meeting. The anger had been diffused and they knew that by the time of the face-to-face meeting they were going there with the intent of 'burying the hatchet'.

Case 5   Theft from sheltered housing

A teenage boy took keys from sheltered housing and stole money.

Ryan moved to the local area with his family in order to live nearer another family relative. This relative resided in a local Scottish sheltered housing complex and the family was fortunate enough to be given the tenancy of a house nearby.

It was not known if he had come to the attention of the police prior to moving to this region. However, since moving, Ryan had attracted the attention of the police for the theft of a bicycle, for which he received a Police Warning.

Ryan was referred to the Reporter to the Children's Panel for breaking into the sheltered housing complex and stealing a considerable amount of money from the office and 6 keys to various flats within the complex. Over the next few days he used the keys twice to enter the flat of a young woman who suffered from learning disabilities and severe sight impairment. He stole the contents of her purse.

Home Visit

When a home visit was undertaken by Offence Resolution Programme staff, Ryan fully admitted the offence and was very apologetic for his actions.

He worked with a Programme worker over a four-week period using a cognitive behaviour, modular programme approach to help him change his offending behaviour. He also agreed to meet with his victim face-to-face, to apologise for his actions and ask for forgiveness.

"Ryan fully admitted the offence and was very apologetic for his actions."

Meanwhile work was also being carried out with the victim, and with her mother as her supporter. Through this dialogue, it became apparent that they also wanted to meet with the young person responsible, to gain an insight into why he had committed the crime and to alleviate their anxiety that he might commit another similar offence.

The meeting

During the face-to-face meeting, Ryan gave an account of his actions and apologised for his behaviour. The victim was given the opportunity to ask questions and to inform Ryan of the consequences and effects his action had on her, and on her mother. The victim's mother also had the opportunity to share her views with Ryan, and how much she had been affected by this incident.

As the meeting progressed, the victim's mother began to ask questions about the juvenile justice system in Scotland, and found it difficult to accept that young people were not punished in the same way as adult offenders. A considerable amount of time was taken up explaining the justice system to her, but she remained extremely angry about the incident and this began to affect the restorative process.

Ryan offered to repay the money to the victim over a period of time. The victim accepted this, but her mother still seemed to require punitive measures to be satisfied with the outcome.

"she remained extremely angry about the incident and this began to affect the restorative process."

There was no compulsion or sanction with regard to the reparation agreement reached, but when Ryan defaulted on his payments, the victim's mother wanted additional sanctions applied. She contacted the Programme to express her disquiet with a system which seemed to advantage the young offender to the detriment of her daughter.

Reflections

- The importance of pre-conference preparation is essential. In this case, it was felt that the victim's needs were superseded by those of her supporter and this possibly made the conference less effective. Although supporters are an essential part of the process, preparatory work may be needed to dissipate some of the raw feelings generated by an offence prior to a conference.

- One of the factors which has led to successful outcomes for the Offence Resolution Programme has been the voluntary participation by young people in a process which seeks to address their offending behaviour. However, this voluntary and educative approach appears, at times, to be at odds with a public perception that punitive action is needed to deal with young offenders.

Case 6   **Damage to a school classroom**

*Four 15 year old boys broke into school buildings
and caused considerable damage. A restorative Justice
Conference took place at the scene of the damage.*

Background

Imran was a 15 year old who lived with his natural parents and younger
brother. He enjoyed a positive relationship with his mother who had serious
health problems, but tensions between Imran and his father had increased
over the last 2-3 years. His father said Imran was a 'model' child until the
age of 12, but felt that his attitude and behaviour had deteriorated
considerably since then. Imran was a very bright boy but his poor school
attendance over the previous 12 months had resulted in Education Welfare
involvement.

Sanjay, also 15, lived with his natural parents and a younger brother and
sister. Sanjay was described by his school as 'underachieving' and whilst not
overtly disruptive, he had a flippant attitude towards schoolwork. Sanjay's
mother was very worried about the people he was currently associating with
and constantly worried about him re-offending.

Sam was a 15 year old who lived with his parents and older sister. There
were no concerns relating to Sam's family or school situation. His current
offence came as a shock to everyone who knew him, and was considered to
be completely out of character.

Karim was a 15 year old who lived with his natural parents, a younger
sister and two brothers, as well as several members of his extended family.
Karim's father was a businessman who employed over 1,000 workers. He
spent long hours working and often travelled aboard. Karim's family's home
was a substantial house in an affluent area. Karim's mother spoke very little
English. Karim was a bright boy but he was under-achieving at school.
Punctuality was identified as one of the problems at school.

All four boys received a Final Warning for their part in two offences of
burglary other than a dwelling. None of them had any previous criminal
history.

The Offence

The young people had been playing football on school premises during a bank holiday afternoon. Two schools (one junior, one high) shared the same site. The boys had found an insecure fire exit at the junior school, entered the mobile classroom used by four-year-old children, and found green powder paint.

Between them they threw powder paint liberally around the classroom, staining floors and ceilings, work top surfaces and some of the children's work on display.

They ate biscuits, which they had found in a desk, stole a small amount of change from the cash tin, and painted nail varnish on the surface of a small cooker used by the children.

The boys then broke a small window on the ground floor of the neighbouring school. One of them climbed in and let the others in. The alarm was activated and all four left the building and began to run away.

Having received a call from a nearby resident prior to the alarm activation, police officers arrived at the scene in time to catch two of the boys, Sam and Karim. Imran and Sanjay were arrested later.

Arrest

All four boys initially denied any involvement in the offences and told a series of lies to the police. They eventually admitted to their individual roles in these crimes and all four received Final Warnings.

During assessments for interventions by a Police Constable from the Youth Offending Service, Karim, Sanjay and Imran expressed remorse, and agreed to take part in a restorative conference with school staff.

Sam lived in another Youth Offending Team (Yot) area and a Police Constable liaised with the Yot. Approximately three hours was spent with each young person discussing the offence and preparing for a restorative conference.

A Police Constable visited the Head teachers from both schools to explain restorative justice principles, and to invite them to take part in a restorative conference. Both readily agreed to take part, and the Head Teacher of the junior school suggested that it might be appropriate for the Teacher of the four year olds in the damaged classroom to take part too. She was invited and agreed to participate. The preparation of these victims took one hour per person.

A date for a meeting was agreed but it was difficult to arrange because the school summer holidays had started and the preferred venue was the damaged classroom. The young people and their families all had holiday plans too.

Sam had been visited by a Restorative Worker from the local Yot, and Sam said he was happy to participate in the face-to-face process, although his parents were not fully supportive of a restorative process. As Sam and his parents were going to be abroad for the agreed date, he wrote a long letter in which he took responsibility for his actions during the offence and offered a sincere apology. Sam knew that this would be read at the meeting by a Yot worker who would be representing him.

> *"each boy gave an account of his involvement in the crime and apologised for the trouble that he had caused."*

The Meeting

The meeting took place just after school in the mobile classroom damaged during the offence. Imran and Karim were supported by their fathers and Sanjay by his mother. They were all nervous.

After introductions each boy gave an account of his involvement in the crime and apologised for the trouble that he had caused.

Sam's letter was read out by a Yot worker.

The junior school Head Teacher explained the impact on the elderly Premises Officer who had been called out by the police on the day of the crime. He had been due to visit his seriously ill sister in hospital at the time, but had to stay to clear up the mess and help to secure the premises. His sister had died that day and he had been unable to see her.

The Head Teacher of the high school explained that, due to the rise in insurance premiums because of the burglary, they had not been able to buy several new computers for the school that had been ordered. These had had to be cancelled. All of the boys had attended this school before moving to their current college.

The classroom teacher gave a most moving account of the impact that their crime had had on the four-year-olds. She told them that they could not understand why someone would want to ruin all their work, which she explained was not just odd paintings but a diary chronicling their progress throughout the school year.

The parents also spoke very eloquently of the shock, shame and embarrassment that they had felt on hearing of their sons' behaviour. Sanjay's mother was very tearful and began to take responsibility for her son's behaviour. The Police Constable reassured her that the meeting did not seek to sit in judgement of the boys or their parents, but to enable them to take responsibility for their actions. This meant apologising directly and trying to understand fully the impact of their offending on those people it had affected the most.

The Infant School Teacher then spoke of a £50 camera that had gone missing and had not been recovered. This had not been spoken about during the preparation period. The Police Constable spoke to the boys and their parents about whether they had any knowledge of this camera. No information was offered. The Police Constable asked whether there were any suggestions as to how this could be resolved. Karim's father suggested that each boy could pay £12.50 towards the cost of the replacement camera.

"She told them that the four-year-olds could not understand why someone would want to ruin all their work."

All parties were in agreement. The Yot worker said she would feed this back to Sam.

This conference was successful in that all three victim satisfaction surveys were returned and were all positive. Three out of the four boys have not re-offended.

Reflections

- Issues that helped the success of this case were the length of the time spent on the preparation of all parties concerned and the willingness of all participants to take part.
- The restorative approach saved the criminal justice system time, money and work in preventing re-offending.

Case 7   Stabbing: a bullied boy snapped, resulting in wounding

A 14 year old male stabbed another boy in the back with scissors after enduring bullying.

Background

Christopher was a slightly built 13-year-old boy. In fact, his appearance was almost identical to the 'Harry Potter' film character, a fact commented upon by most people who knew him!

Christopher had been the subject of several instances of bullying at his school, and this had begun to affect his health and life in general. Christopher's parents had reported the bullying to the school, and although attempts were made to prevent re-occurrences, this did not prove very successful.

The bullying took the form of verbal taunts inside and outside school, of a personal nature. These taunts were extremely hurtful to Christopher and he was struggling to cope with the stress that it was causing him.

The Offence

One afternoon, during a science class, one of his 'not so regular' tormentors, Steven, began to tease Christopher in a way that Christopher felt would end in the usual taunts.

In Christopher's own words, at this point, 'something snapped'. He picked up a pair of scissors from a nearby desk, and lunged at Steven's back, cutting through clothes and piercing the skin near his shoulder blade. Terrified at his own reactions, he ran from the classroom and away from the school premises.

Christopher had not planned any of these reactions, and was unsure of what to do next. Living in a rural town, Christopher walked through fields for a long time, until it got dark. He returned home late evening to frantic parents who had contacted the police and reported him missing from home.

In the meantime, the police had been called to the school, and had taken statements from Steven and witnesses. The scenes of crimes service had been busy taking forensic samples, and Steven had been taken to the local hospital by his mother, Ruth, who was a Teacher on duty at the same school. Steven's injuries turned out to be minor, but would have been very serious if the scissors had punctured a lung.

Charges

The police deliberated as to whether to charge Christopher (who was of previous good character) with wounding – a very serious offence. After taking all of the facts and history into account, plus a statement from the victim requesting leniency, a decision was taken to give Christopher a Final Warning.

Christopher was excluded from the school for an indefinite period, to be reviewed on a regular basis by the Head Teacher. Following the Final Warning assessment, Christopher was referred for short-term intervention work to address his offending behaviour.

A referral was also made to the Youth Offending Service Restorative Justice Worker. The reason for the referral was to consider a Restorative Conference. This was at the request of a very remorseful Christopher, and supported by his parents.

Restorative Conference

During the Restorative Conference assessment, Christopher expressed deep remorse for his actions, and was anxious to explain to Steven that the incident was not planned and that he had reacted irrationally for reasons not connected with Steven.

Christopher did not want to discuss the bullying with Steven, as he did not wish to be seen as a 'wimp' or to minimise the seriousness of his crime.

Christopher's mother, Debra, was quite tearful during the assessment, but totally supported her son's commitment to a restorative justice conference. After the trauma of these events, she was glad to have a reason to feel proud of Christopher once again.

I then contacted Steven's mother, Ruth, and arranged to visit. During my visit, Steven was very quiet, although he listened intently to the explanation of the restorative process, and Christopher's version of events.

He readily agreed to take part in a restorative conference.

Ruth, however, was less convinced of the merits of such a meeting, and doubted the sincerity of Christopher's remorse, but agreed to support Steven, as he clearly wanted to take part. After spending two 2 hour sessions with both parties, the meeting took place in the Inspector's office at the local police station. This office was pleasant and airy, and the venue was the preferred option of Steven, and Christopher was comfortable with this.

Christopher expressed deep remorse for his actions, and was anxious to explain to Steven that the incident was not planned and that he had reacted irrationally for reasons not connected with Steven.

During the meeting, Christopher described the events with amazing eloquence, pleasantly surprised his tearful mother, and clearly moved Steven and Ruth.

Although Christopher did not make reference to the persistent bullying that he had suffered at the hands of some other students, it was clear that he had been driven to his drastic action by a great deal of pressure, and his remorse showed that this was obviously very out of character for him.

Steven, to the amazement of all present, especially Ruth, responded by saying "I'm sorry if anything I said made you do that."

This was a very brave statement by Steven, which clearly indicated that he had been aware of some of the pressure that Christopher had been under, due to the stress caused by bullies. The chemistry between the boys changed at that moment from distant tension to mutual empathy.

Debra gave an emotional, but very poignant account of the impact that this had had on her and the rest of the family, and reinforced her son's remorse. Ruth had been visibly stunned by Steven's response to Christopher, and was only able to say a few words about how it had affected her and her family.

"I'm sorry if anything I said made you do that."

The meeting was closed, and Christopher and his mother looked relieved and happy. I asked Ruth and Steven to remain after the others had left.

Ruth could barely contain her anger towards her son. She said that she had felt humiliated that Steven had lied to her about the fact that he had not taken any part in bullying Christopher. This, she felt, had reflected on her abilities as a mother and a teacher.

Steven left us for a short time of his own accord. I assured Ruth that far from reflecting negatively, this process had shown that she had a son who was prepared to do the right thing at a time when it was so important to Christopher, knowing that it would make his mother feel the way she did at that moment. What Steven had done showed great courage, and therefore deserved praise for his honesty. Ruth eventually saw this point of view, and, when Steven returned, she ruffled his hair and gave him a hug.

The contents of this meeting, with permission of all concerned parties, was related to the Head Teacher. As a direct result of this, Christopher was allowed back to school very soon after, and settled back well into school life. He has not re-offended, and I believe is unlikely to.

Reflections

- Despite meticulous planning, unexpected events can still occur (e.g. Steven's admission to some level of bullying).
- This case highlights the importance of debriefing all concerned.
- The conference was successful as it 'cleared the air' between both boys, and the offender's school exclusion was waived as a result of this process. This success is judged by feedback from debriefing, and the school's Head Teacher.
- Planning and preparation assisted the success of this case.

Case 8   **Burglary of a factory**

*A group of boys broke into factory, damaged
machines and lit a series of small fires. The
factory owner accepted the apology and offered
one of the boys a job if he stayed out of trouble.*

Damien was a 10 year old boy with learning difficulties. He attended a mainstream school and had a statement of special needs. He had no previous criminal history, but was easily led by older boys. His parents, although shocked by this crime were caring and supportive of Damien.

One Sunday afternoon, Damien, together with a small group of boys known to him (two as young as 6) and some older boys of 13 crawled inside a hole in a wire perimeter fence of a large factory which manufactured wooden staircases. The group managed to enter the factory via one of the main doors, which had been ajar.

Once inside, the boys began to ransack the factory floor. They smashed a food and drinks machine and ate most of the contents. Some of the older boys then began to light small fires with matches. Damien insisted that he had not been responsible for lighting the fires, and that he had in fact tried to put them out. The fire alarms were activated, and the boys were arrested when police arrived, at the same time as the fire brigade.

Damien was given a Final Warning by the police for his part in this offence of burglary. Following assessment by a Youth Offending Team worker, Damien was assigned a volunteer from the Youth Offending Teams' Intervention Team. He agreed to receive six weekly visits to work on issues relating to his offending behaviour. One such visit concentrated on victim awareness. During this session, Damien asked whether it would be possible to apologise face-to-face to the factory owner. The Intervention Team Manager contacted a Police Constable in the Youth Offending Team.

The Police Constable visited Damien at home with his parents. During the assessment, Damien was asked what he wanted to say to the Factory Manager. His initial reaction was shy, nervous laughter and an apparent inability to explain his actions.

It was gently pointed out to Damien that if a meeting was to be set up with the Factory Manager, who was a very busy man, he would not be very happy if Damien was unable to speak to him.

Damien suddenly began to give a lengthy and very convincing account of his actions during the crime. He explained how they had entered the factory, broke into the food and drinks machine, exactly what he had eaten and drunk, what he had broken and ransacked, and how he had tried to put out the fires lit by some of the others.

Damien's parents told me that this was exactly the same version of events that Damien had told them and the police. The Police Constable asked Damien if he thought he would be able to tell the Factory Manager what he had just said. Damien said he would.

The Police Constable then contacted Phil, the Factory Manager, and explained the principles of Restorative Justice to him. Phil readily agreed to meet Damien. The Police Constable visited Phil in his office above the factory floor. This was to be the venue for the meeting. The Police Constable spent just over an hour with Phil, the same length of time spent with Damien.

For the meeting Damien was supported by his father, James, who, although keen to meet Phil, was very nervous. Phil greeted us and showed us to his office. Damien seemed fascinated to see the factory floor in full operation.

Damien listened intently to Phil's side of the story.

During the meeting, Damien again gave a very full and frank account of his own actions during the offence, for which he took full responsibility. He did not try to minimise what he had done, and afterwards gave a heartfelt apology to Phil. Both Phil and James were visibly moved by Damien's genuine sincerity.

Phil thanked Damien for asking to take part in the meeting. He acknowledged his courage and accepted his apology. Phil then went on to describe to Damien his shock and horror on seeing the mess and damage caused to the factory. He explained the financial impact on the company, not only from cleaning up the mess, but from the loss of a day's production, and the cost of replacing damaged goods. Phil also told Damien that he had sacked the security guard on duty on the day of the offence. He also described the impact of the crime on the rest of the staff. Damien listened intently to Phil's side of the story.

Phil then asked Damien how old he was. Damien had just had his eleventh birthday. Phil asked Damien whether he thought he might like to work in a place like his factory. Damien nodded furiously. Then, to the surprise of Damien and James, Phil offered Damien a job at the factory when he left school, providing he stayed out of trouble. Damien was delighted, James was choked with emotion.

Then, to the surprise of Damien and James, Phil offered Damien a job at the factory when he left school, providing he stayed out of trouble

Then came the turn of James to speak. He told Phil that he and his family were not used to dealings with the Police. In fact, when the Police arrived to tell them about Damien's part in this offence, they first thought they had come to tell them that he had been involved in an accident. He described the shame and embarrassment of his son at the police station, but then balanced this with the pride that he felt when his son showed the courage to take responsibility for his actions. James also thanked Phil for his amazing offer of employment for his son.

Everyone present was thanked for their contributions, Damien suddenly asked Phil if he could show him the points of weakness in the factory's security and where they had managed to crawl through the fence. A site tour then followed, with Phil making notes of Damien's observations, with a view to significantly improving the overall security of the inside and out of the building.

Damien has not re-offended.

Reflections

- This meeting was very successful, judged by the positive response from Damien and James during the de-brief, and the very positive victim satisfaction survey returned by Phil.
- Issues that assisted the success of this case were the willingness of both parties to meet, and the thorough preparation of all parties prior to the meeting.
- Although meetings usually take place in a neutral place, managers of businesses and shops are mostly too busy to attend, unless people go to them. Sometimes there is also positive merit (as in this case) in going back to the 'scene of the crime'.

- The restorative approach saved the criminal justice system time, money and work as Damien has not re-offended.

Case 9   Assault following longstanding tensions

A girl assaulted another girl with a vodka bottle. Both girls saw themselves as the victims.

There comes a moment in many Restorative Conferences when the facilitators seem to vanish. It's as if the two protagonists, the 'victim' and the 'offender' are alone in the room. The hurt that has come between them has been exposed, and both parties are anxious to close the gap and find a way towards healing. The process is now theirs, and the facilitators, who have been holding the ground between them, fade into silence.

Jodie and Marcia had fallen out years ago, and the bitterness spilled over into violence one night, when Marcia struck Jodie on the head with a vodka bottle. Jodie was rushed to hospital where she was treated for a deep gash. Months later she was still suffering severe headaches on that side of her head.

Marcia had insisted before the conference that Jodie had struck the first blow, and denied having drunk alcohol prior to the offence. I visited both families at home in preparation for the conference, and I was anxious that the conference might dissolve into dispute about facts Those fears were ungrounded, largely due to the way restorative conferences work.

At the outset of the conference I asked everyone to speak honestly and truthfully, to respect and listen to one another, to focus more on what they were thinking and feeling at the time and the impact since, not so much on what they had or hadn't done.

It was moving to witness these two teenagers sorting it out for themselves.

There comes a moment in many Restorative Conferences when the facilitators seem to vanish.

Marcia admitted for the first time that she'd been drunk that night. She apologised several times to Jodie, and said how shocked she was that she was capable of such an attack. She then thanked Jodie for not pressing for prosecution. The case might have warranted a court sentence for Grievous Bodily Harm, but was dealt with by a Final Warning.

It was moving to witness these two teenagers sorting it out for themselves.

The transformation came when Jodie herself began to apologise. She admitted that she had listened to and believed the rumours and gossip going around about Marcia. She acknowledged that Marcia had been having a hard time at home.

Both girls said that the divisive name-calling and general bitchiness of their 'friends' had led them into conflict, and both were now determined to put an end to it. They took the first courageous step to resolve these issues, in a process that transforms adversaries into allies, and does away with the mentality of 'victim' and 'offender'.

About five months after the conference, I was asked by the Youth Offending Team Manager to invite some people who had been involved in a restorative process to a Youth Offending Team event. I was delighted that Jodie and her mother wanted to come (Marcia and her mother said they would have liked to attend but weren't available). Jodie said that as a result of the restorative conference she now felt safe, and was able to meet Marcia in passing without fear or anxiety. They wouldn't ever be friends, she said, but they could now get on with their lives.

I consider the meeting to have been successful, based on the response of the victim's and offender's families when contacted five days after the conference, and the both girls' feelings several months later. And to our knowledge the offender hasn't been charged with another offence.

Reflections

- The case was assisted by the fact that both girls entered the process voluntarily, and with a common desire to sort out their problems and avoid further incidents.
- This is a case where both girls saw themselves initially as victims. The conferencing process was able to handle this in a way that the court process cannot.

Case 10   **Criminal Damage to a Church**

*Three boys (aged16-17) broke church
windows and wrote offensive words around
the church door. Reparation was carried out.*

Background

Three 16 and 17 year old boys were sitting in a churchyard one sunny
Sunday afternoon, slightly bored and with a catapult. They started to aim
stones at the windows of the church, small diamond leaded paned windows
and broke quite a number of them. One of them wrote some offensive
words around the church door. The Curate had seen them and the police
were called. All three were charged with criminal damage and given Final
Warnings.

This was the only green space in this neighbourhood, a deprived inner
city area. With the knowledge and consent of the Vicar, the church grounds
were used by many people to enjoy the peace and quiet and appreciate the
mature trees. Children also played there and the church hall was used by
many groups, including mother and toddler groups, pensioners' and
women's groups. Many people took great pride in the church which was
very old and beautiful. Until then there had been no damage. The damage
and the writing upset many people, especially the older ones who saw the
church as an important and central part of the community, a community
they had seen deteriorating quite severely in recent years.

After the Final Warnings, the boys were referred to Restorative Justice
to see what could be done in this case.

Restorative Justice Intervention

I made contact with the Vicar and the Curate of the church and discussed
with them at some length the various options. They were quite willing, in
fact eager, to meet with the boys and discuss the impact on the community,
which was substantial. They also wanted the opportunity to express their
views directly.

The boys had not considered any of the consequences of their actions while they were doing what they did, and had not thought much about it since. For one of them the most disturbing thing had been that the police still had his hooded jacket and bandana which they had kept for evidence.

However, after a long discussion with me, they accepted that there might be a wider view and all agreed to meet with the Vicar and the Curate. The mother of one of the boys was particularly upset as this was the church in which she and his father had got married, and where her son had been baptised. She was wholeheartedly in support of the meeting.

We arranged a mediation session at the church hall and I agreed to pick up all three boys and bring them to the church. The meeting went well, with all three boys listening closely to the Vicar and thinking about what he and the Curate said. They apologised and explained why they did what they did, and the one boy even owned up about his links with the church. The boys agreed with the Vicar and the Curate that they would come back to the church and do some weeding and ground work. I had told the boys not to wear their usual trendy clothing and particularly not the bandanas. They all came smartly dressed and clearly very anxious to make a good impression.

We arranged the reparation session after consultation with the elderly gentleman who kept the grounds in good order on a voluntary basis. It was a very hot sunny day and unfortunately they took to heart my comments about their clothing a little too well. None of them had even thought to bring a hat to protect their heads, so I had to lend them the ones belonging to my children that were in the car – which did not please them as my children are very young! They worked *The boys agreed with the Vicar and the Curate that they would come back to the church and do some weeding and ground work.* very hard for 3-4 hours, weeding and clearing ground so that broken grave stones could be laid flat. We even had to move some toads that were living under one of the broken grave stones – actually I had to do that – the brave teenagers could not bring themselves to touch them!

Members of the community saw them there, asked what they were doing and were very pleased when they were told.

This piece of restorative justice has restored a community, given the boys the chance to be reintegrated (the ban on them entering the churchyard has been lifted), allowed them the opportunity to apologise and be forgiven, and allowed the victims and the community the opportunity to express their views and receive reparative work. A very good result for work over an eight-week period.

Reflections

- The preparation undoubtedly affected the outcome and also that they knew I was going to supervise them. Quite a rapport had built up while I was doing the preparation work and I think it would have been harder, particularly in one case, to get the boys there if I had passed the case on to someone else.
- At the time of writing, two of the boys had not come back through the criminal justice system. The third one unfortunately has, but due to personal circumstances. He became homeless and his last offence was around these issues.
- In this particular case, the reparation activity worked well and was well within the health and safety guidelines.

Section 3

Preparation of pre-sentence report

Case 11   Disorder Offence: Offender was a victim; Police Officer becomes victim; how was humanity regained?

A woman in her forties was drunk and disorderly in police station and needed to explain how much despair she felt after her last encounter with the Criminal Justice System

Jenny, a woman in her forties, walked into the police station and was drunk and abusive, expressing her anger with the criminal justice system in ways that led to her being arrested and charged with disorder. Whilst the Probation Officer was working on writing a pre-sentence report for the court it became clear that she wanted to express to the Woman Police Constable (Alison), who arrested her, what had led up to her being so abusive. A mediator was contacted and it was noted that the local police force had already reached an understanding about enabling police officers to attend mediations as individual victims of crimes.

A couple of sessions were spent with the offender (Jenny) letting her talk her way through the horrendous experiences she'd had. What Jenny wished to express was the depth of her despair at how lightly the criminal justice system had treated the physical and sexual abuse she and her daughter had suffered from her ex-partner, Dave. Following his being given only a short custodial sentence, Jenny's daughter, Anne, frightened that the sentence was so short and fearful of Dave, committed suicide. Jenny blamed both Dave and the criminal justice system for her death. The day after Jenny was contacted by the probation service (after Dave had served just a few months' sentence) to be told that only half of the prison sentence was being served by Dave, she got drunk and went to the police station to vent her anger.

The mediator spoke to Alison, the victim of the disorder offence about whether she wanted to hear from or talk to Jenny. She both wanted to understand what had provoked the incident and to explain what her job was when such behaviour occurred at the police station. First Alison felt the need to contact her senior officer who was happy for a mediation to go ahead.

The joint meeting

The meeting was held in the Family Court Welfare Office which was regarded as a neutral venue, very close to the police station in question and close to where the offender lived. The mediator introduced Alison and Jenny, explained that Jenny (the offender) had asked if this meeting would be possible and that the victim (Alison) agreed to it. I had already explained to Jenny that I would ask her to speak first at the meeting, which I did. And they just took it from there and took 2 or 3 hours to talk it through.

Jenny explained that she doesn't normally behave like that. She got very emotional and told the Police Officer that she'd gone out and got herself into a state that night. She explained how she felt about the fact that Dave was coming back out of prison. Jenny explained what had happened to her daughter and it was fairly clear that it had been a struggle to get over that. Alison expressed that she was very pleased to both have met Jenny in the context of a mediation and to have found out what it was all about.

Alison explained that she had no alternative but to arrest Jenny on that night. Once she had arrested her there was no way that anything could have stopped the progression of the paperwork. So she explained the reality of the system in relation to this offence and what would inevitably happen if Jenny did anything like that again. Alison said it must seem grossly unfair. Alison agreed that prosecutions for a series of sex offences – such as Jenny and Anne had been victims of – often didn't acknowledge the full extent of the offending that had been committed against them. Alison said that the police often shared a similar frustration in that they work hard and put cases through the courts and then feel that they have been let down by other parts of the system.

Jenny fully accepted that there was nothing else that Alison could have done that Saturday night, and her concern was that she didn't want to leave her mark as being the dishevelled, disorientated, abusive person who had appeared in the police station lobby that night. She wanted to leave a different impression. She wanted to explain that in the light of sober reality she knew that she couldn't, and didn't want to, accuse this police officer of anything but she did want Alison to know why she had felt the need to go into a police station like that.

In summary an explanation of the offending was given and accepted, and an explanation about the system was also given in the other direction. They came to terms with the reality even though the offender still felt let down by the criminal justice system in relation to her ex-partner.

The one specific request from Alison was that she wanted to receive news of the court case outcome, as this information would not usually come to her. The mediator let Alison know that she would keep her informed.

The outcomes

• In terms of the pending court case, it was known to both victim and offender that the outcomes of the meeting would be reported back to the court and there was some discussion of what words would be used. The case went to court for this offence alongside another couple of offences which were also associated with Jenny being unable to cope with what had happened to her as the victim of severe abuse and violence. Jenny was sentenced to a two year Community Rehabilitation Order, which was geared to assist her to begin to find a way out of the difficulties that were giving rise to offences.

• The mediator saw the offender after the court case and also relayed news of the sentence to the victim. She checked that they were OK and that there was nothing further that they wanted to exchange between them.

• The mediator kept in contact with Jenny until about six months into sentence, where she just checked that everything was OK. The offender wanted the police officer to know that she was a lot better and doing reasonably well on the order. The police officer wanted Jenny to know that she hadn't forgotten about it all and she still sent her her best wishes. Alison hoped that Jenny would be able to get a lot more out of her life than she was getting.

• This mediation was a stage in helping Jenny to look at different ways of dealing with her anger.

• The mediation process achieved what every mediator values in terms of humanisation. The dehumanising elements of criminal justice (lack of work with victims) were both the cause and substance of the restorative work.

Reflections

- A local understanding that police officers have rights as victims to participate in victim-offender mediation helped progress the case. It could have gone ahead without a senior's approval. Mediation meetings have been facilitated by this mediator working with social workers, medical workers and police officers as victims whose seniors opposed their involvement. Fore-thinking what the professional issues could be is sometimes important.

- The case was dependent on the actual personality of the officer. A lot of officers feel that they shouldn't participate because they've got to uphold a certain authority.

- Proper preparation for this mediator involves "trying to do all that can be done so that by the time you've got to the meeting the predominant emotion isn't anger."

> *"trying to do all that can be done so that by the time you've got to the meeting the predominant emotion isn't anger."*

- The mediator thought the offender had been wronged and thinks it is important that we don't try to change people's fundamental views that they'd been wronged. People's dignity is at stake, and sometimes, giving them a better understanding of how something happened, is best done respectfully, without undermining anyone's dignity.

- The mediator thinks that sentencers made a much better decision than they would have done without the information from the mediation.

- Existing law towards victims is deficient. "I believe all cases should come to us anyway to explore what role mediation might play."

- Everyone involved in a crime should have the opportunity to go through this sort of process. The mediator's suspicion was that embarrassment and the pressure of the next case were factors that caused the only dialogue with Jenny after her abusive partner's sentence to be a notification of the sentence and the question as to whether she wanted to be informed when he'd be released. Jenny was terrified of him being released as was her daughter: "No doubt the person would have offered to put her in contact with a counsellor but certainly in this part of the country, even if she did that today, you could wait for longer than the sentence for someone to become available."

- The mediator saw this as valuable both in terms of seeing people properly as victims but also the not uncommon confusion about labels. That people don't generally conform to the labels we put them into. They're simply convenient markers. But once you get into any restorative process the labels become immaterial.
- It may be not a very big success, but in general the success for us is hopefully about making a life change which is more important than if people re-offend or not.

"I believe all cases should come to us anyway to explore what role mediation might play."

Case 12   Robbery of an Elderly Woman

Two boys (aged 14 and 15) robbed an elderly woman's handbag and knocked her over causing shock, distress and injury.

The Offence

The offence happened while the victim (Florence Smith) was returning from the shops. She was robbed and knocked to the ground by two boys. Her bag was taken but recovered soon after. She received painful bruising to her legs and a blow to her head as she fell, and was understandably very shocked and shaken. The offence left Florence fearful for her safety, and a local neighbour (Nicola Jones) who witnessed the entire incident took care of her.

The two offenders were arrested soon afterwards. Ian and Brian were 15 and 14 years of age respectively, both attending the local school, from which they often truanted together. Both had special educational needs. Ian had never been in trouble with the law before and Brian had previously received a Final Warning for some minor offences. The robbery was not planned in advance – its purpose was to gain some money to pay off debts incurred for buying soft drugs. They intended no harm to Florence and had not meant her to fall during the bag snatch.

Brian pleaded guilty immediately, and the case was heard at Crown Court because of its seriousness. He was given a 12 month custodial sentence (Detention and Training Order). Ian, however, pleaded not guilty and had to attend an identity parade, where he was identified by Florence's neighbour, Nicola. At this point he changed his plea to guilty, and when sentenced (later than Brian) received the same sentence as Brian – a 12 month DTO.

Ian (but not Brian) had been referred to the Family Group Meetings (FGM) project immediately prior to his appearance in Crown Court. He had been assessed as suitable, but it was not known at that stage whether the victim would be interested. However, while in custody, Ian was in too much of a state to discuss the matter any further.

"When I heard the impact of the offence on the lady I decided that I could never do anything like that again."

In cases where offenders receive a sentence of one year or more for a violent or sexual offence, a Victim Contact Worker from the Probation Service contacts all victims. On a second visit an FGM facilitator accompanied her. Florence said she had a number of specific questions that she wished to ask both young men and she particularly wanted them to know the impact of the offence on her. She wanted to attend a face-to-face meeting with one of the two young men, with Nicola Jones (her carer and witness) as her supporter.

The FGM project facilitators had been disappointed that Ian's case could not be dealt with in the community, especially as the victim wanted some contact with the offenders. They were also disappointed that Brian had not been referred. However, despite this, they were able to take forward preparations for Family Group Meetings when the offenders were released.

Family Group Meeting with Brian

When Brian was due for release, another FGM facilitator went to see him. He was willing to attend a Family Group Meeting and preparations were made for this to take place as soon as he was released. The meeting was held in a local community centre; Florence and Nicola attended as did Brian, his mother and a worker from the Youth Offending Team.

Florence was able to say very clearly and forcefully how she had been affected both physically and emotionally. Nicola was also able to say what effect the offence had upon her. This was very difficult for Brian and his mother to hear, and many tears were shed. By the end of the meeting a plan was agreed to support Brian to avoid any further offences and a genuine apology was offered and accepted.

Family Group Meeting with Ian

Ian, having initially pleaded not guilty, had been sentenced some months later than David. His sentence was the same length as Brian's and he was released under supervision after half of the sentence. When Brian was due for release, another FGM facilitator went to see him. On a final visit as part of his pre-release preparation the FGM was finalised and included as part of his Training Plan.

Florence and Nicola didn't attend this meeting, but their opinions were voiced via a Victim Impact Statement. Ian opened the meeting by producing a letter of apology that he had written to Florence. Ian was thanked for this, but it was explained that part of the purpose of the meeting was to enable him to understand more fully the effects of the offence on the victims, and it would be more appropriate to offer an apology after having gained that understanding.

The meeting reminded them that Florence and Nicola had both suffered as a consequence of Ian's actions. Nicola was especially concerned that Ian's initial denial had put her through the trauma of an identity parade and she was angry about that. Ian explained that he was so ashamed of what he had done that he could not tell his family and so denied it at first. He was very sorry to have put Nicola through the ordeal of attending the identity parade.

A Family Plan was made around supervision and support, the input from the Youth Offending Team, frequency of contact and the resumption of formal education/training. It was agreed that the first session would be for Ian to rewrite the letter of apology in the light of what he had heard. This took place the following week. By the end of the session Ian had turned a cursory two-paragraph letter, focusing primarily on his own experience, into an individual letter to Florence and another to Nicola, addressing the specific issues and questions they had raised. The letters were taken in person by the FGM facilitator and the Victim Contact Worker to Florence and Nicola.

Letters of apology

Dear Mrs.Smith

I had a family meeting last week. The statement you made was read out, the statement was hard to listen to for me and my parents. Made me think how badly you was affected, I understand physically you had banged your head, forgetting things, bad legs, lost weight and affected sleep. And emotionally scared of young people and maybe another attack, and maybe feeling isolated from society and lonely. I am very sorry what happened that day and regret it deeply, Me myself has never been in any form of trouble myself apart from that time and never again. In the family meeting we discussed my future, I want to go into computers and stay out of trouble, I have started a course already. I don't understand why we did it but I do try and it will never happen again and I am sure of that. The action we took was so wrong and it will be in my head for the rest of my life. Hope you can go back to your old routine, and feel safe again. I will write to your friend and explain my apologies.

Sorry Ian.

Dear Mrs Jones,

I was in a family meeting last week when Mrs Smith's statement was read out it, was hard to hear because of all the problems she's had. I have written a letter to Mrs Smith, it must be hard for you to see your friend not happy. I am sorry you had to go to the I.D parade and that I would not admit to the offence. I didn't admit to it because I was scared. I knew I could of got into a lot of trouble and I would say I did in the end. Also scared of what my parents would think of me. I've never been in trouble before and I was confused and scared. Sorry for putting you through that. I have made a plan for the future, which is hoping to go into computers, I have started a course now. Once again I am very sorry.

Sorry Ian

Ian's comments about the process

Later Ian talked about how he had found the process.

"It was helpful; at first I didn't want anything to do with it, I 'd done my punishment."

"When I heard the impact of the offence on the lady I decided that I could never do anything like that again."

"The process was made easy for me by giving me choices that I could make."

When asked if he would recommend the process to others, he said:

"If you feel guilty, then do it, it will really sort your head out, it really helps to say you're sorry."

"If you feel guilty, then do it, it will really sort your head out, it really helps to say you're sorry."

Reflections

- The two offenders were both involved in Family Group Meetings, but in different ways to accommodate the wishes of the victims.
- Good quality work was undertaken pre-sentence with one of the offenders.
- Whilst the victim was an elderly and frail 88 year old, no assumptions were made about her willingness or appropriateness to participate in the process; she was visited and in a sensitive and respectful way her views and concerns were listened to and taken into account.
- The case was patiently worked through for nearly 12 months to enable a successful outcome; however, the system does not always allow such a generous time scale.
- The letters of apology produced by Ian after hearing and understanding just how Florence and Nicola had been affected were much more comprehensive and meaningful than the token effort he had produced prior to the meeting.

Case 13   **Street robbery at knifepoint**

A 15 year old boy was robbed by two boys
who attended the same school. Following a
meeting, a detailed agreement was made.

Gavin, a young person aged 15, was stopped in the street by 2 young people. One of the young people produced a small knife and the other asked Gavin to give them his money. Gavin handed over £5 and the two offenders ran away. The two young people were charged with the offence of robbery and had to appear at the Youth Court.

Paul aged (16) pleaded guilty to the offence of robbery. The magistrates asked for a pre-sentence report (PSR) to assist them in sentencing Paul. During the court adjournment period, the PSR author referred Paul to the project.

Paul had a previous conviction for shop theft and had lived with his older sister for the past year due to a breakdown in relationships between Paul and his parents.

A Project Worker visited Paul and his sister Catherine to assess his suitability and explain the process of victim-offender mediation (VOM). Paul was initially wary of the process but willing to accept responsibility for his actions by meeting the victim. However, once the worker had reassured him that his safety would be protected, Paul gave his informed consent to participate and Catherine agreed to be his supportive adult at the face-to-face meeting.

The Project Worker then visited Gavin and his mother Karen to consult them about the opportunity to take part in VOM. Gavin was keen to participate because he knew Paul lived in the local community, attended the same school and that they would probably meet at some time in the future. Karen said she was slightly worried about Gavin meeting Paul and the VOM process. She asked for 24 hours for her and Gavin to think about this. Subsequently Gavin gave his informed consent to participate and Karen agreed to be his supportive adult.

Sentencing at Youth Court

The Project Worker submitted an assessment to the court, confirming Paul's suitability, and that Gavin and Paul had both agreed to participate. Paul was sentenced to a 12 month supervision order, with a condition that he should participate in VOM, with up to six contacts with the VOM service, subject to the continued agreement of the victim to participate. Gavin was free to leave the process at any stage.

Preparation Work for RJ Meeting

Two project workers visited both Gavin and Paul with their carers and undertook an in-depth preparation session. The workers explored what both young people wanted to say at the meeting and what they wanted to get out of the process. The workers also re-visited the ground rules and the process of the meeting and the role of the supportive adult.

Face-to-Face Meeting

The meeting took place in the early evening at a local voluntary sector building two weeks after Paul had been sentenced to his supervision order. The two project workers used the five-stage model of engagement of mediation to assist Gavin and Paul to consider the impact of the robbery and its implications for the future.

i) Engagement: Gavin and Paul gave their perceptions of the offence. How it affected them at the time and their concerns about the future.

ii) Issues: Gavin and Paul explored and clarified the issues the offence had caused and might cause for both of them in the future.

iii) Options: Paul and Gavin looked at what options they had to address the issues they both identified. Catherine and Karen were asked to contribute to discussions about the last 3 points of the agreement.

iv) Agreement: A formal written agreement was produced outlining how the issues and options would be dealt with.

The Agreement

1. Paul wanted to apologise to Gavin for the effect of the offence upon him. Paul did this during the meeting and Gavin accepted his apology as genuine.

2. Paul and Gavin agreed to treat each other with respect if they met in the community. Their definition of respect meant being polite and not swearing or assaulting each other.   *Paul and Gavin agreed to treat each other with respect if they met in the community*

3. Gavin did not want Paul to communicate with him or to approach him at school. Paul agreed that he would not approach Gavin at school.

4. Gavin wanted Paul to agree not to re-offend against him the in the future. Paul said he would not re-offend against Gavin in the future.

5. Paul wanted Gavin and his friends to agree not to offend against him in the future. Gavin agreed that he would not offend against Paul in the future. Gavin said that he could not accept responsibility for the actions of his friends but he agreed to try his best to prevent them from offending against Paul.

6. If Paul or Gavin had any problems with each other they agreed to tell their own supportive adult, Catherine or Karen, the same day a problem happened, so that they could help them sort the problem out.

7. Catherine and Karen agreed to contact each other on the same day Paul and Gavin reported a problem, in order to try and help Paul and Gavin sort the problem out.

8. Karen and Catherine agreed to swap phone numbers immediately after the meeting to help with the 2 points above.

v) Feedback: 3 weeks after the mediation had been completed, Gavin and Paul were interviewed by a researcher from a local university as part of the monitoring and evaluation of the project. The project was in the process of establishing a multi-method approach to monitoring and evaluation of VOM. This included the following elements:

- Restorative – satisfaction of offenders and victims with process and agreements
- Rehabilitative – rates and types of any re-offending by offenders
- Retributive – did the offender find the process and outcomes easy or difficult?

Reflections

- Working in partnership: The Youth Offending Team worker who referred Paul had made the cultural transition of incorporating restorative approaches into their case management of young offenders. The Youth Offending Team worker and other professionals felt that the combination of restorative and rehabilitative methods were of benefit to the victim and the offender.

- Issues to be resolved: Gavin and Paul both had issues to be resolved from the offence and the repercussions of it for the future.
- Supportive adults: Paul and Gavin both had supportive adults willing to engage in the process and be part of the options and agreements stage of VOM.
- Training and experience: The project workers were accredited mediators. One was also a qualified social worker, the other a former probation officer with extensive experience of working with young people and their carers.

Section 4

Serving a community sentence

CASE 14 Theft from store

A boy stole a computer game from a large store.
Following a meeting, the Store Manager offered
the offender a work experience placement.

Robert stole a computer game from a large store in town. Having recently left his job, he had intended to sell the game to get cash. As he had a Final Warning for a previous offence, he had to appear in court for the first time, and received a Referral Order. As part of this, he was referred to the victim-offender mediation service, which undertook preparations with victims and offenders for panel meetings.

The mediator contacted the victim, who had taken part in (indirect) mediation before and was pleased to have the opportunity to be involved again. The mediator had also contacted Robert, prior to the referral panel date, during which, it was discovered that a close relative had died the previous day. She notified his Youth Offending Team worker so that they could offer support and encouragement. It was important to ensure that Robert didn't feel so overwhelmed that he didn't turn up for the panel meeting, now that the victim had made special arrangements to be present.

The mediator met the victim to discuss the panel procedure and what sort of reparation work (if any) was sought. At the referral panel, the victim explained the cost of theft to stores nationally and how the knock-on effect meant fewer jobs and higher prices. She also spoke of the risk to the staff, as they were unable to tell, when tackling a shoplifter, whether any weapons or syringes were being carried. She said what a gamble this was for everyone, but particularly for a 16-year-old Saturday person, earning just £4.50 per hour.

She also spoke of the risk to the staff, as they were unable to tell, when tackling a shoplifter, whether any weapons or syringes were being carried.

Robert apologised to the Store Manager and told her how embarrassed he was and how he had been 'shamed up' in front of his mates. He said it wouldn't happen again. He spoke of his ambition to work in the RAF and realised that that would be impossible with a criminal record.

Accompanying Robert was a Princes Trust worker, Carol, who explained to the panel how Robert was engaged on a 12 week course with them. She gave a detailed account of the competition for each place on the course and told them how well Robert was doing. She informed the panel that the next step in the course was for Robert to work full-time for two weeks in a local business.

The victim had decided that she wanted a window painted in the store as the reparation work. However, when she learnt of Robert's involvement with the Princes' Trust, she immediately offered him a 2 week work placement at the shop.

She said she had made up her mind within 5 minutes of meeting Robert, that he was a decent lad who had made a mistake that he was now sorry about.

She said she had made up her mind within 5 minutes of meeting Robert, that he was a decent lad who had made a mistake that he was now sorry about.

The panel agreed to make it a special case and allowed him to do it. Robert was delighted. The chair of the panel stressed to him the importance of behaving in the shop and that a lot of people were putting their faith in him. He said he wouldn't let any one down.

Before he left, Robert shook every one's hands and thanked them.

The mediator made sure that the victim didn't feel under pressure to offer the 2 week placement, but she confirmed that, on the contrary, she was pleased to have the chance to help Robert. She felt 2 weeks might be long enough to impress on him how the shop operated and in any case, she wasn't short of work that needed doing. She hoped that by allowing Robert to do his reparation work at the place of the offence, he would feel pride in the shop, thus preventing re-offending. Convicted shoplifters are normally banned from the victim's shop so she was really showing great generosity on her part.

The mediator contacted the store manager during the 2 week placement to ensure everything was going well. The victim was pleased with Robert's work, in fact the arrangement had gone so well, she wanted to write a job reference for him.

A successful conclusion!

The panel members spoke of it being 'the best panel' they had attended, as it was so constructive and communication had been so open and forthcoming.

A relationship of confidence and trust had been nurtured between the victim and the victim-offender mediation service, which led to the willingness of the victim to partake in a 3rd case.

The victim was pleased with Robert's work, in fact the arrangement had gone so well, she wanted to write a job reference for him.

Reflections

- Undoubtedly, the fact that Robert had enrolled on the Princes Trust course and earned the respect of the Princes Trust support worker, inclined the victim to have direct contact with him. Had Robert not been remorseful for his offence nor made an effort to contribute to society in a positive way, whether voluntarily (on the Prince's Trust course) or otherwise (he had enrolled at college to study the necessary A-Levels to enter the RAF), the victim would have been less likely to have offered the work placement.

- Allowing Robert and his supporter the opportunity to tell the panel of his present circumstances and future objectives led to the victim considering her own approach to the crime and offering something positive. This was beneficial for both victim and offender.

CASE 15 Indecent assault on sisters' best friend

The Family Group Meetings Project
explored the possibility of a face-to-face
meeting between victim and offender.

The initial referral was made in January. Robert, aged 14, had committed an indecent assault on Laura, his sister's best friend. At court, he was given a 12 month Referral Order. The local protocol indicated that in addition to an adolescent sex offender risk assessment (called an AIM Assessment), the Family Group Meetings (FGM) Project would explore the potential for a face-to-face meeting of those affected by the offence.

The offence had occurred at Robert's house. The AIM (assessment) report, written by NSPCC workers, noted that Robert had no previous history of offending and saw the offence as occurring within the context of exploratory adolescent behaviour. Robert desisted from the behaviour once Laura became upset and had showed remorse towards her for the harm caused. Robert felt he had a 'boyfriend-girlfriend' relationship with Laura and the assault took place within that context.

Laura was very upset and distraught by the offence and immediately told Francesca, Robert's mother, who told Robert off and calmed Laura. She asked Laura what she wanted to do and Laura said she wanted to forget it and not tell her mother.

It was some weeks later that she disclosed the details of the offence to her father who immediately informed the police. Robert was arrested and charged. He co-operated with the investigation and made no attempt to deny the offence although there was some disagreement about the extent of the assault.

The AIM assessment tool divides offenders into quadrants according to strengths and risk, and the team does not accept offenders with low strengths and a high risk of re-offending, because of the possibility of re-victimisation. The AIM assessment showed Robert as having 'low to moderate' risk of further offending, with some strengths and resilience which boded well for ongoing work, despite poor social skills and special educational needs. Finally the report noted parental inconsistency in setting boundaries, exacerbated by the fact that Robert's care was shared between his father John and his mother Francesca, who had been living separately since Robert's early childhood.

Contact with Robert and his family

The AIM Assessment was not completed until mid February, so the first visit to Robert and his parents by the FGM project took place in the first week of March at John's house. The meeting laid out the potential for an FGM and explored Robert's attitude to the offence and its consequences. Robert was very quiet and shy, and easily overwhelmed by his very vocal and easily provoked mother. John stood quietly in the background and listened to what was said. Francesca felt strongly that Laura bore some responsibility for the offence and justified her decision that day, not to contact Laura's mother. Time was given to allow them to think about involvement in the process.

Subsequent visits built rapport and a sense of trust with Robert, which enabled him to talk in his own words about what happened. From this it became clear that he was placed in the almost impossible position of accepting responsibility for the offence with the support of his father, but having to reconcile this with his mother's view, which placed far more responsibility on Laura and was very defensive in approach.

In the end a Referral Order Panel date was set for April and Robert's father attended. Neither the victim nor her mother attended the meeting but Susan; a Victim Contact Worker employed by the Youth Offending Team, attended and gave a brief account of the victim's views. As part of the contract it was agreed that Robert would continue with the FGM process on a voluntary basis.

Contact with Laura and her family

The first contact was made with Laura and her mother Julie also during the first week in March. Laura appeared to have recovered from the initial trauma of the offence and although offered support from Social Services, had not felt in need of it. She 'wanted to put it behind her' and get on with her life. For her, the greatest repercussion of the offence had been the disrupted friendship with Paula, Robert's younger sister. The facilitators explained the FGM process and its voluntary nature, and emphasised their independence. Time was given for them to think through the potential and possibility of a meeting.

Two weeks later a follow-up visit was made, and both Laura and her mother expressed an interest in following the process further. We began to explore the points they both wanted to raise and the questions they wanted to ask. It was agreed that Laura's father, who was estranged from the family, would not be involved, mainly because of Laura's mother's feelings. After two further visits a summary of points and questions was drawn up. Finally everyone agreed on a set of ground rules for the meeting.

Preparations for the FGM

After the Referral Order Panel meeting, we were able to focus the FGM on the benefit of communication between the 'two sides'. This identified exploration of the aftermath of the offence from both perspectives, looking at questions about motives and the impact of the offence on Paula's and Laura's friendship. (This had continued but was under tremendous pressure). The facilitators emphasised the 'future focus' of the meeting and ground rules to enable respectful and effective communication.

I was very keen to involve Francesca, as she was a major 'opinion former' within her family, and her views were largely based upon her own view of how she would respond if she were in Laura's mother's place. Francesca's volatility and unwillingness to move from her fixed interpretations of the past made preparation very difficult. We had individual sessions with Robert and his father, since Francesca took over family sessions and spoke on behalf of Robert imposing her own confrontational views.

We tried to work with her identified 'short fuse' and agreed a strategy with her to manage this during the meeting. But just before the meeting Francesca failed to be available for the ultimate visit. She phoned to cancel the meeting because Robert was scared of her reactions. A visit was made to Francesca on her own, and it was agreed that she wouldn't attend the meeting but a statement and series of questions would be presented on her behalf.

All this raised Robert's fears, and these were addressed by re-emphasising the ground rules and making a strong commitment to his physical and emotional safety.

Professional preparation

In addition to the discussions with the referrer (the Referral Order Co-odinator) two meetings were held with Robert's Youth Offending Team Caseworker. She was on holiday on the day of the FGM but agreed to provide a report detailing her concerns and the resources available to the Youth Offending Team.

Robert co-operated fully with the requirements of the Youth Offending Team and engaged with the NSPCC staff who were following the intervention plan outlined in the AIM assessment. The other important issue identified by the Youth Offending Team worker was the need to re-integrate Robert back into full time education. He had been out of school for two and a half years, despite being subject to a statement of special educational needs, and his family was very concerned. The offence further complicated attempts to get him back into school. Accordingly the Youth Offending Team worker referred him to the specialist Education Support Worker in the team, and also to a mentor to support Robert in structuring his considerable free time more positively.

The Education Worker was away for a week, and the victim and her mother agreed to delay the meeting. The Education Worker (who had previously attended another FGM) was prepared by phone but we held a face-to-face meeting with the mentor to explain the process and the ground rules. In total it took from March to June to complete the preparation, about 35 hours work.

The meeting

The meeting was held on a Saturday morning. The venue was originally a local community centre – however, the week's delay meant we had to rearrange the venue and use the local victim support office.

Participants

- Laura, victim of offence
- Julie, mother of Laura
- Robert, young man who committed the offence
- John, father of Robert
- Dave, Youth Offending Team Education Worker

- Steve, Robert's mentor
- Two facilitators
- Apologies from Pauline, Robert's Youth Offending Team worker who was on leave.

Structure of the meeting

It was agreed to stick to the usual 4-part structure of a Family Group Meeting, that is:
1. Victim–offender dialogue
2. Youth Offending Team concerns
3. Private planning time for the family
4. Recall to approve plan

However a number of changes were needed to make the meeting more applicable to the specific circumstances of this case, these were:

- The victim–offender dialogue was broadened out to consider who had been affected by the offence and how, the questions this had raised for them and their wishes for the future. We also recognised that the usual requirement of a detailed account of the offence might be difficult for the victim and her mother to hear in the company of others. Respecting this wish for sensitivity presents the danger of 'glossing' over the offence and thereby excusing the behaviour. We decided therefore to focus upon the effects and impact of the offence rather than the mechanical detail of who did what.

- It was also important to maintain a strong future focus as all participants cited a desire for things to be better in the future as a key motive for involvement in the process. To achieve this, the questions from the facilitators were framed in four temporal frames, 'How was it at the time?', 'How has it been since?', 'How is it now?' and 'How do you want it to be?'

- We agreed in preparation with all participants that we would only refer to people by name and avoid damaging short-hand labels such as victim and offender; although participants did talk about the offence which occurred.

- We supported the participants in speaking with their voice about their story. They are the experts in their own lives and have the potential to 're-story' their futures and to be surprised by hearing the realities of others.

How the meeting went

The meeting began with thanking the participants for being present, as their very presence at the meeting was indicative of a desire and willingness to listen to others, as well as having their story heard. The ground rules were stressed in a positive way. This was particularly important in view of the concern about anger of others expressed by Robert's family. At the end of the meeting, the facilitators commented that difficult issues had been voiced in a way which showed that anger was not the only means of reacting to the offence. This was a very powerful message for Robert, especially as his father John had been able to explore his and others' emotional reactions without raising his voice or losing his cool.

Both Laura and Julie were able to make powerful statements about the impact of the offence, within the four temporal frameworks, and identified their wants for the future. Laura wanted to be able to resume her friendship with Robert's sister Paula, and also wanted to feel safe when she inevitably encountered Robert in the community or at Paula's home. In response, Robert was able to articulate who had been affected by the offence and how. His first thoughts were about the impact on himself and his family, but with further reflection was able to realise and recount the effect on Laura and Julie. He voiced a quiet and powerful direct apology to Laura and Julie, which they acknowledged and received. Moreover he was able to say directly to Laura that she would be safe in his company.

The meeting also created an action plan for Robert. Whilst much of the professional input related to support for Robert, this balance was redressed by John, who said at the end of the meeting, 'We have heard a lot to do with Robert in this meeting but I would like to ask something about Laura.......' . He went on to enquire about Laura receiving help and support for the effects of the offence and expressed a concern that this should be available. Julie quietly thanked him for asking the question.

Reflections

- This case indicates that Restorative Justice can have a valuable role to play with regard to sexual offending. Indeed the specific circumstance of this case is 'typical' of many adolescent sexual offences.
- The victim was younger than the offender and previously known to him.

- There was a need to negotiate future contact which would guarantee personal safety for the victim.
- Social relationships were disrupted for the wider social network; the victim and offender were at the centre of this but parents, friends and others were critically affected too.
- Language can be problematic when describing sexual behaviour; we tried to use the participants' language as much as possible.
- Assessment is vital in the area of sexual offending, as meetings may only be appropriate in some cases.
- The assessment process should identify positive strengths as well as risk factors, to give a more balanced view.
- The relationship of the Restorative Justice process to the 'intervention' programme needs to be thought through. We are committed to being independent and neutral regarding the responsibility for casework with the offender. For this reason facilitators do not pass on information, as this would compromise the independence of the facilitators and undermine the process.
- This case shows that there are real benefits for both parties from the process that the conventional criminal justice process is largely incapable of delivering, such as the apology and the assurance of safety. Cynics may cast doubt on the benefit of this and want a 'statutory mandate' to back it up. However, the offender's apology was made in the company of his family, the family of the victim and professionals – an 'audience of accountability'.
- The time scales of Referral Orders makes victim engagement difficult, especially when detailed assessment and preparation are necessary before a face-to-face meeting can be safely offered. Yet adolescent sex offenders are included in Referral Orders, making this one of the few restorative interventions to address these issues. We estimate that between 1-3% of cases will be sex offending. Few, if any, Referral Order Panels are skilled or resourced to cope with this and fewer still have the potential to 'outsource' a quality Restorative Justice provision such as a Family Group Meeting to offer a restorative process.
- Finally, the meeting provided a model of dealing with difficulties without resorting to conflict, enabling a 're-storying' of the problems.

CASE 16 Aggravated taking without owners' consent – an angry victim

A 16 year old boy stole a camper-van and crashed it. The angry victim was dismissive about mediation but eventually agreed to meet the offender.

16 year old Terry was referred for a mediation assessment after being sentenced to a Community Rehabilitation Order for Aggravated Unlawful Taking of a Motor Vehicle. He was the youngest son in a fairly large family of high achievers. The family enjoyed a comfortable life-style in a favoured village just outside a small town and his parents could not understand Terry's behaviour. Terry had been with friends in town on a Saturday night and in the early hours of Sunday morning he had stolen a camper-van from outside a private home and attempted to drive it home. He lost control of the vehicle, swerved into a ditch and crashed into a tree. Terry had been hospitalised for several weeks. The experience had given him time to consider his position and analyse his own behaviour. When the mediator met him he was keen to enter the mediation process, but he did not want his parents to accompany him. His parents gave their consent.

The mediator met the owner of the vehicle, Mr Johnson, at his business premises in the town. Mr Johnson was still furious, even though several months had elapsed since the offence. The police had given him information on the offender which, in the course of time, had been considerably exaggerated by the victim. At first Mr Johnson was dismissive about mediation, stressing how dangerous it would be, because he would not be able to control himself. However, he kept asking questions and the mediator decided that indirect mediation might be the best way of helping the two parties. Over a period of 6 weeks,

At first Mr Johnson was dismissive about mediation, stressing how dangerous it would be, because he would not be able to control himself.

the mediator made frequent short visits to the victim, giving new pieces of information from or about the offender on each visit, with the offender's family's permission. Finally, Mr Johnson decided that he wanted to meet the boy, even though he believed that he could never forgive him and would be unable to view him dispassionately. Despite that information, Terry and his family agreed to the meeting.

The mediator chose a safe environment for the meeting in an office equipped with a panic button and with a security guard on duty in the building. When Terry walked into the room Mr Johnson quickly got to his feet, went straight to him and shook his hand. Although the mediator had anticipated no real threat from Mr Johnson, she was surprised at the generosity of his reaction. Mr Johnson congratulated Terry. He believed that very few boys would have had the courage to attend such a meeting. The pair talked for over an hour covering many topics and Mr Johnson felt that Terry's apologies were sincere. Mr Johnson explained how the loss of his van affected him and his family: he used it to collect goods from manufacturers and wholesalers, to make deliveries to customers and to take his wife and two young children on holidays. Their summer holiday had been cancelled because the van was a write-off and, due to the court case, there was an insurance hold-up. Terry offered to do whatever he could to make amends for the upset he had caused. Mr Johnson said he would consider the offer. Mr Johnson was keen to find out about Terry's life and what had caused him to offend. He was eager to give advice and help 'put him on the right track' in order to become a happier person and have a successful life.

He believed that very few boys would have had the courage to attend such a meeting.

On a follow-up visit to the victim, Mr Johnson told the mediator that he had had time to reflect on his own feelings, the meeting and Terry's offer. He said that, following the offence, he had been outraged and he had, unwittingly, passed those feelings on to

He said that, following the offence, he had been outraged and he had, unwittingly, passed those feelings on to his two young children who were now very scared of the stranger who stole their camper-van.

his two young children who were
now very scared of the stranger who
stole their camper-van. Mr Johnson
felt guilty that his children were so
fearful and wondered if Terry would
be willing to write a letter to help
reduce their anxiety.

*...they no longer felt he was a
'nasty man' and their fear had
dissipated. The letter had been a
complete success and the children
had been delighted with their gifts.*

Terry was keen to help and gave
much thought and time to the exercise. He enjoyed the company of his
young nieces and nephews and thus was able to relate easily to young
children. He suggested, as it was now close to Christmas, that he would like
to enclose a present for each of them with the letter, if Mr Johnson agreed.
Mr Johnson was pleased by the offer but insisted that any present should be
of small financial value. During two sessions the mediator watched Terry
compose and write the letter so that she would be able to guarantee to Mr
Johnson that the letter was entirely his own work. Terry then went
shopping with his girlfriend for age-appropriate gifts. The mediator
collected the Christmas parcel and delivered it to Mr Johnson. On the final
visit to him in January she discovered that he had read the letter to his
children on Christmas Day and their reactions to it were splendid; they no
longer felt he was a 'nasty man' and their fear had dissipated. The letter had
been a complete success and the children had been delighted with their
gifts.

This case was extremely successful for the offender and the victims and
they all verbally expressed their satisfaction with the outcomes. The
offender believed that he had done all that he could to help the victims
recover from the offence and, therefore, he felt a little less guilty and more
able to contemplate a return to 'normal life'. He was surprised that the
victim had been so kind to him at the mediation meeting and reflected
often on the advice he had been given; the experience had helped him
mature. The victim was pleased that a very negative experience had been
neutralised by the mediation process and had even turned (slightly) into a
positive outcome.

The offender's parents were proud that their son accepted full
responsibility for the offence and were pleased that he was courageous
enough to attend a mediation meeting. Consequently the relationship
between the offender and his parents improved following the restorative

intervention and this was a contributory factor in helping the offender to re-establish his position in the community and prevent any further offending.

Reflections

• Safety of participants is of paramount importance and, therefore, it was useful to have a safe environment for the mediation meeting, accessible at short notice and available outside normal office hours.

• Indirect mediation proceeded at the victim's pace and this provided the opportunity for the participants to devise creative, customised reparative agreements.

• Until a guilty plea had been entered, only one of the parties could be contacted by the mediator in order to avoid contamination of evidence if a trial had ensued. Thus, protracted cases where, perhaps, a Newton Hearing is involved, means that the participants are sometimes prevented from obtaining a restorative justice intervention at the time they most require it.

CASE 17 Criminal damage to a vehicle

*A 17 year old jumped along the roofs of
vehicles when drunk, causing £2,800 of
damage to an Alpha Romeo.*

Max was 17 and, out celebrating with a friend, got drunk, jumped along the roofs of several cars, causing considerable criminal damage, including to an Alfa Romeo. This car was four months old – too new to scrap – and the repair bill was £2,800. Needless to say the victim was very angry and frustrated with the pointlessness of it all and very inconvenienced.

Max appeared in court for criminal damage and was given a 3 month Referral Order. Max told the Referral Order Panel that he wanted to apologise and the Youth Offending Team Police Constable referred him to the Mediation Scheme at his own request, agreed by the Panel. Max also took part in some community reparation events, including a sponsored swim to raise money for a local charity.

We visited Max first at home. Being 17 he was able to choose to see us alone. He had not involved his parents in the case at all, feeling very ashamed and needing to see himself as coping with the consequences of his actions.

During the visit lasting about 1.5 hours we talked through with Max the consequences for himself, his future, his family and especially for his victims – who of course were unknown to him. He expressed real regret and a firm wish to apologise face-to-face. He decided to write a letter of apology saying how much he wanted to meet to give the apology in person. He wrote a good and sincere letter which we took away with us.

Two cars had been severely damaged. One of the owners did not want to meet us or go forward to mediation. The second one did. We then had to wait for victim details from the Youth Offending Team who, for data protection reasons, must make the first contact. After about a fortnight we were given a name and address which was out of date, so there was a delay of about a month.

The victim, Trevor, was reluctant to see us but willing to talk on the phone. He agreed to receive the letter by post and contact us again to let us know if he wanted to meet. However, we had to make the follow-up call. Trevor still wasn't sure he wanted to meet Max. He said the letter was fine as far as it went – but was it genuine? After much discussion he agreed to meet at a neutral venue.

The face-to-face mediation was very successful, judged by the changed attitude of the victim by the end of the meeting. Hands were shaken and good wishes exchanged.

To prepare Max for the mediation we met with him beforehand to talk him through what he might say and how he would cope with the anger which might be expressed. He was determined to go ahead although nervous. We also met with Trevor to help him think through what he might say. We were assessing each party to ensure that this would be a safe situation and were convinced it would be.

The face-to-face mediation was very successful, judged by the changed attitude of the victim by the end of the meeting. Hands were shaken and good wishes exchanged, but not until a fair amount of anger and frustration had been expressed honestly though not abusively.

Max accepted the responsibility for what he had done. He didn't use drink as an excuse – indeed he stressed that drinking too much is also an offence which he didn't intend to repeat. His obvious regret did eventually get through the anger and frustration of the victim, but both agreed that it couldn't actually take away the damage done.

Trevor began to ask Max about himself and his future, gave him some advice which he said had been learned the hard way and they both talked freely about moving on and what that meant to them. There was a real sense of closure for both. Both completed mediation evaluation forms most positively at a later date.

Both victims received some financial compensation. Max paid a sum of money towards this.

Reflections

- Issues assisting success were the offender's true remorse and wish to make a face-to-face apology. A good letter of apology helped to pave the way, also persistence on the part of the mediators.
- The need for the Youth Offending Team to make all first approaches meant a very lengthy wait for the Mediation Scheme.
- This mediation nearly failed because we were given old contact information. A lot of time was wasted, trying to making contact with the victim, and this was very time-consuming.
- This mediation could easily have failed because the victim was still angry and cynical, so was reluctant to invest his time in a meeting.

CASE 18   Public order offence following a final warning for a similar incident with the same victim

A 16 year old male was involved in an incident with a 16 year old boy who was known to him in a local park. The offender had already received a Final Warning for an assault on the same victim.

Michael was an intelligent, articulate 16 year old who had just left school and was waiting to join the armed services. He presented as an athletic and muscular lad, but it later became apparent that he had previously been overweight and this had been a source of discomfort and embarrassment for him in the past. Michael lived in a semi-rural town that had little in the way of leisure facilities for young people. Consequently the local youths often used a local car park as a social venue.

One summer evening Michael made his way to the car park with Richard, a friend of his. Upon arrival they saw a group of youngsters, one of whom was a lad that Michael had assaulted 12 months previously – a local 16 year old called John. On the previous occasion Michael had punched John in the face, breaking his nose, and had received a Final Warning for the offence. At the time John had maintained that the assault was unprovoked. Michael never gave a detailed reason for hitting John. Michael had simply stated that John had wound him up and he'd lost his temper.

Assault

Michael claims he approached John on this occasion with the intention of talking to him. However, things did not go according to plan and there was some pushing and shoving, which resulted in all the lads present becoming involved in scuffles. During the melee Richard, (Michael's friend), assaulted John. Richard punched John in the face, knocking him to the ground, and left him lying there in a dazed state. Richard later received a Reprimand for this offence. Michael was caught up in a tussle with another lad and was not involved in the assault on John but when he saw John on the floor he went over to check whether John was alright. Michael was stood over John trying to talk to him, when Richard again approached. He stood behind Michael and kicked John in the ribs, leaving him with severe bruising.

Referral Order

Following extensive police enquiries, 3 months later Michael was charged with a public order offence and the Court sentenced him to a 3 month Referral Order. As is the normal procedure with Referral Orders, a Youth Offender Panel (YOP) was arranged and the parties involved were contacted.

Because of John's age, his mother, Mrs Jones was telephoned by the Youth Offending Team (Yot) Victim Officer, with a view to obtaining her permission to discuss the case with John and invite him to attend the YOP. Mrs Jones replied that she wanted to talk to John herself first and she arranged to call back a few days later. When Mrs Jones did call back it was to say that John was happy to put forward comments about the incident but he'd decided not to attend the YOP in person. He was very frightened of Michael and found the prospect of seeing him far too daunting. Instead of attending himself, John had asked his parents to attend the YOP on his behalf.

Mrs Jones said that her son wanted to know why Michael had assaulted him and added that he desperately needed reassurance that Michael would leave him alone in future.

The Victim Officer then discussed the matter with Mrs Jones over the telephone. It quickly became apparent that John believed the kick he'd received whilst he'd been lying *Mrs Jones said that her son wanted to* on the ground had come from *know why Michael had assaulted him* Michael. The Yot Victim Officer informed Mrs Jones of the facts *and added that he desperately needed* that had been accepted by the *reassurance that Michael would leave* Court but she did not really believe them. Mrs Jones stated *him alone in future.* that John had been feeling quite vulnerable and wary of Michael ever since the first assault had taken place. This second incident had confirmed his worst fears and had left him feeling very distressed. She told the Victim Officer that John barely left the house for several weeks after the second incident, as he was so terrified of bumping into Michael again. Mrs Jones said that her son wanted to know why Michael had assaulted him and added that he desperately needed reassurance that Michael would leave him alone in future.

John barely left the house for several weeks after the second incident, as he was so terrified of bumping into Michael again.

Michael's Yot Case-worker was informed that Mr and Mrs Jones wished to attend the YOP and asked to discuss the matter with Michael. The Yot Officer telephoned Michael and it became apparent that Michael was disappointed John would not be attending in person. Michael told his Case-worker that he had wanted to explain to John that it wasn't him that had assaulted him in the second incident, though he did feel some responsibility for the fact he had been assaulted. Michael said he wanted to apologise to John and let him know he had no intention of going anywhere near him again. Michael was comfortable with the prospect of John's parents attending the YOP and hoped they would be able to relay things to John on his behalf.

The Meeting

The Youth Offender Panel took place a month after Michael's Court appearance at a neutral venue in a neighbouring town. As the meeting started the body language of those present suggested to the panel members that tempers may be about to fray. Michael, to his credit, appeared quite open and relaxed but his father seemed rather distrustful and defensive. Mr and Mrs Jones (John's parents) also seemed slightly hostile, and there were a fair number of glares being exchanged between both sets of parents.

The Jones's mood did not improve when they listened to Michael's version of events, they firmly believed that Michael had assaulted John and did not believe him when he denied this. There was quite a lengthy exchange on this issue which the panel members were tempted to interrupt, but they were glad they had allowed the discussion to flow when Mr Jones announced that Michael had convinced him of his innocence. Michael's father looked sceptical at this but Michael visibly relaxed when he realised he had been heard and his story had been accepted.

At this point Michael felt confident enough to raise the issue of the first assault on John. Although this offence was not part of the current case he acknowledged that it was, in some ways, connected. He fully admitted his actions, making no attempt to minimise the events or make excuses for his behaviour. Mr Jones then read out a statement John had given him to bring to the Panel. In it John talked about how distressed he had been feeling and how many problems his nose injury had caused him. Michael looked very ashamed whilst he listened to Mr Jones and immediately volunteered an apology. This came across as utterly genuine and, at that point, the Jones's smiled and visibly relaxed. Seeing them respond in such a positive way reassured Michael's father and he too appeared more relaxed.

The Jones's accepted Michael's apology but asked him to explain why he'd assaulted John. Mr Jones commented that John had told him he'd done nothing to provoke Michael in any way, but added that he wasn't naïve enough to believe that John hadn't done anything at all.

Michael started by simply stating that John had wound him up but, when pressed, it transpired that John had been teasing Michael for many years regarding his weight. Michael had endured name-calling and taunts from John until on that occasion, he snapped and hit John. At this point Michael stated that he recognised using violence was not the way to respond in such situations and readily acknowledged that he could have dealt with it differently.

Mr and Mrs Jones agreed with Michael that he had responded inappropriately and said they couldn't condone his response but they also went on to acknowledge that he had been sorely provoked and John had been wrong to treat Michael the way he had. They apologised on his behalf, saying that they couldn't condone his behaviour either and would speak to him about it when they returned home.

The Jones's then asked Michael why he'd not left things alone after the assault, and why he'd approached John in the car park to talk to him. They suggested to him that it was a decision that was always likely to result in trouble. Michael agreed with them and said he regretted ever going over to speak to John. He said he had no intention of ever going near John again, not even to talk to him. Initially Michael seemed reluctant to explain why he'd felt he needed to talk to John on this occasion but, again, when pressed he revealed that it was to ask John to 'call off' his older brother Chris.

It transpired that, ever since the assault on John, Chris had been intimidating Michael, following him around and threatening to beat him up for breaking his brother's nose. Michael told the panel that he had been feeling very frightened by this and said he'd just wanted to ask John if he could ask Chris to leave him alone. Mr and Mrs Jones looked horrified by this disclosure. They immediately apologised to Michael and assured him that they would talk to Chris about his behaviour as soon as they returned home after the meeting.

The panel meeting then went on to discuss issues of reparation (a letter of apology and some community work) but it was clear that the restorative work had been done during the course of the discussion and further reparation was not particularly important to the participants.

Reflections

- This meeting was successful because the Jones's had had an opportunity to tell Michael how John had been left feeling as a result of the two incidents and they had also been able to ask Michael questions. Both were things that were very important to them.

- In response, Michael's free acknowledgement that he'd behaved inappropriately and had made some bad choices, together with his voluntary apology and assurance that he would leave John alone, were exactly what the Jones's had hoped to hear. Michael seemed relieved to have had a chance to clear his name (with the Jones's) about the second assault on John, and was pleased to have been able to apologise for his actions. Michael also seemed relieved to hear that the Jones's would speak with both of their sons regarding their behaviour towards Michael. These were issues that were important to him.

- The Panel had the courage and confidence to allow the discussion to flow but, at the same time, had the judgement to know when to interrupt. Good mediation skills were essential to this process.

- This approach may have saved time, money or work from the point of view that the actions of the two Jones lads might never have come to light if it hadn't been for this meeting. Without their behaviour being addressed there may have been a danger of further incidents involving

Michael. Michael accepted that he'd not dealt with things appropriately but, if he hadn't been given an opportunity to tell anyone what had been happening and ask for John's parents' help, he may have resorted to inappropriate behaviour in the future.

- The existing laws and guidelines relating to Youth Offender Panels sometimes make it difficult for them to work in a truly restorative way. Normally for a meeting to have a chance of being restorative it is reliant upon the young person being willing to attend. Sometimes this will be the case with Youth Offender Panels but often the young person will be there simply because they have to be and the dynamics will not be the same.

- John's parents were satisfied with the Panel process and outcome but they were not satisfied with the service they got from other justice agencies. They felt they had too much of a struggle with the Police and Crown Prosecution Service to have the case taken to Court in the first place, and they felt let down by this.

- Good communication was essential to this case. There is a need for greater emphasis upon the practical communication skills rather than the theory.

CASE 19   Assault on a peer

A 12 year old boy assaulted a fellow pupil
after a history of classroom bullying.

Martin was a 12 year old schoolboy. He was into the usual things for a boy of his age – in particular – 'nu metal' music, and he wore various t-shirts with band logos such as 'Linkin Park' etc to reflect this interest. His image drew attention to him – some of it unwanted – and he was subjected to name-calling. This had been happening for about 2 years.

Louis, also aged 12, started picking on and bullying Martin whilst they were both in school. Louis would name call, push and dig Martin in class, trying to get a reaction out of him, so that he would retaliate, have a fight and end up getting in trouble from the teacher.

Louis also stole various belongings of Martin's such as lunch boxes and pencil cases, which Martin found very distressing. Louis broke several pairs of Martin's spectacles and it cost his parents money to replace them.

The offence

On the day of the offence, Martin was playing in a park with friends near to his home, when Louis and a group of youths approached Martin from behind. They called him names before physically assaulting him. Martin was too frightened to retaliate, so said nothing and tried to walk away. Louis punched Martin in the eye and kicked him about the ears and body.

When he returned home, Martin told his parents what had happened and they contacted the Police.

Martin had sustained injuries including bruised and swollen eyes and ears. He also suffered from headaches, sleepless nights, nightmares and a lot of nervous tension, which manifested itself in mood swings and bad tempers. Martin did not suffer any of these problems prior to the assault.

To help Martin deal with the situation, his mother enrolled him in Judo Classes to use his nervous energy constructively. Martin also missed 3 weeks of school, as he was afraid of reprisals, and more bullying.

The outcome

Louis was given a 3 month Referral Order for the assault and was referred to the Youth Offending Team (Yot) for intervention.

Martin was contacted by the Victim Liaison Officer to invite him to have his views recorded and to be involved in the Youth Justice Process, and a home visit was arranged. Martin and his parents were interviewed, and their views were recorded. They agreed to Direct Reparation in the form of a letter of apology, and Indirect Reparation in the form of a community task. They also attended the Referral Order Panel Meeting where it was identified that both parties would volunteer for victim-offender mediation. This was arranged by the Youth Offending Team, and the Victim Liaison Officer, Louis' Case Manager and an outside Facilitator were present at the mediation.

A further home visit was made to Martin to prepare him and his family for the mediation.

The whole process from the case being allocated to mediation taking place and closing the case took 3 months.

After the mediation, both parties were invited to complete an evaluation sheet regarding the process and both answered 'very satisfied'. Martin wrote "It was very helpful and it helped me understand the matter more than I did before".

"It was very helpful and it helped me understand the matter more than I did before"

The meeting was followed up with a phone call to Martin, and the case was then officially closed.

Reflections

• This case was a very successful one in that the victim was given the opportunity to have his say and be heard. Without mediation, the victim may have had a lot of unanswered questions.

CASE 20 Assault with actual bodily harm

A 15 year old girl accused a fellow school pupil of spreading rumours and then assaulted her causing actual bodily harm.

This case concerns Tracy who was the subject of a 6 month Referral Order in respect of an assault (Actual Bodily Harm) on another 15-year-old girl, Samantha who attended the same school. The case had been transferred to the Youth Offending Team (Yot) from a neighbouring larger county authority. The transfer was required due to the fact that Tracy was in a foster placement in a seaside town (where the offence took place). The placement had broken down (as a result of the offending behaviour) between the offence being committed and attendance at the Youth Court.

A Referral Panel was set up and the victim and her mother invited to attend. Prior to this meeting Tracy was interviewed at her new foster placement to produce a report for the panel and to inform and prepare her for the forthcoming panel meeting. In tandem with this, an appointment was made to visit Samantha and her mother to explain the Referral Order process and prepare them also for attendance at the panel meeting. Also invited were Tracy's Social Worker and her birth mother.

Panel Meeting

The panel meeting did not get off to a good start, as the victim Samantha was very agitated and nervous. This would be the first time she had seen Tracy since the assault and she was fearful of further violence. The start was also difficult for Tracy as her Social Worker had to inform her that despite promises given, her birth mother would not be attending. This resulted in an angry outburst from Tracy.

Samantha outlined what had taken place and how she had been affected by the assault. She had been accosted on the way home from school by Tracy and a group of her friends. Tracy had screamed at her that she, Samantha had told lies about her then started hitting her until she was knocked to the ground, at which point several of the others present also started kicking her.

After the assault, Samantha had to receive medical attention at hospital for a number of injuries. Her clothes were torn and her mobile phone was broken in the attack. As a result of the assault, Samantha had not felt safe to go back to school and would not leave her home for fear of meeting Tracy. In effect her life had gone on hold.

Samantha had not felt safe to go back to school and would not leave her home for fear of meeting Tracy. In effect her life had gone on hold.

For her part Tracy explained that she had been told by another girl that Samantha was supposed to have put around slanderous rumours about her. However she had not sought to validate these accusations and had attacked Samantha on the spur of the moment feeling she could not back down in front of her friends. Tracy genuinely appeared to be quite shocked to hear of the effect on Samantha of the attack.

Outcome of the Meeting

After both Samantha and Tracy had explained what had happened on the day, the meeting moved on to drawing up a contract that would assist Tracy to prevent further offending, make reparation to Samantha and give her some assurances around further possible contacts. Tracy was able to apologise to Samantha for the hurt that she had caused and to assure her that it was very unlikely that they would ever meet by accident as they now lived in different areas and if they did there was no possibility of another attack. Furthermore Tracy agreed to pay out of her pocket money for the repair of Samantha's mobile phone on a weekly basis. For Samantha the most important aspect was that she could leave her house and return to school without fear of further attacks. It gave her a sense of closure in that she was now able to move on and resume a normal life again.

In the case of Tracy it was an important move forward for her in that she took responsibility for her actions, admitted that she had acted wrongly and now had a clear understanding of the effects her actions had had on Samantha. For her also it was a case of being able to move on and learn from the experience.

Reflections

It is often easy to dismiss an assault perpetrated by one young person upon another as unimportant. This case clearly demonstrates the wide-ranging effects that the assault (which could almost have been dismissed as a 'playground brawl') had had on the victim. By bringing together both victim and offender there was a chance to bring a closure to the matter for both parties, particularly in the case of the victim who was able to receive assurances from the offender that enabled her to pick up her former life again. The process had also given the offender the opportunity to take responsibility for her actions and make amends to some degree.

CASE 21   Burglary of a family with young children

*A 13 year old boy burgled a family home,
causing fear and distress to two young children.*

A 13 year old male appeared in court and received a 9 month Referral Order for burglary. The Victim Liaison Officer contacted the victim to see if they would be interested in being involved in any Restorative Justice process. While the Youth Offending Team Case Manager was contacting the offender to complete an assessment and explain the process, the Victim Liaison Officer made contact with the victims and arranged a home visit.

The victims

The victims were a family consisting of Mum, Dad and 2 children aged 7 and 11. They were extremely traumatised by the burglary. The offender had entered their home via the children's bedroom window and had taken toys, a video recorder, video films and a play station with the games. The children were scared that the 'monster' would come back for them. They refused to sleep in the bedroom (a difficult situation as the property only had 2 bedrooms) and needed a light on constantly.

The children were scared that the 'monster' would come back for them. They refused to sleep in the bedroom…. and needed a light on constantly.

The Dad was angry, as they were not insured and he had no way of accessing the money to replace the items taken. The family took some time to consider whether they wanted to meet the offender at the Referral Order Panel meeting but telephoned 5 days after the meeting with the Victim Liaison Officer to say that they would like to attend.

The meeting

The meeting was held at a time and a place convenient for the victims i.e. a local community centre on a Saturday morning. Initially the Mum and Dad were to attend but in the event, the Dad arrived alone, saying that the Mum was too nervous to come. The offender arrived with his Mum and Step-Dad.

After the initial introductions, the Panel Leader asked the offender to explain how he had come to commit the offence, how he felt about it now and what had happened since. The offender explained that he had been told by a gang from school that if he committed the burglary he could become a member of their gang. They had waited outside the property for him and had taken the items as soon as he had emerged.

The offender displayed no obvious emotion at this time. The victim listened. The Panel Leader then asked the victim to explain how the offence had affected him and his family, how they felt and what had happened since.

As the victim explained the fear and upset that had been caused, particularly to the children, the offender began to cry. He expressed his sincere remorse and asked if he could meet the children to apologise and explain that he was not a 'monster'. This offer was declined but a dialogue developed between the victim, offender and parents and it was agreed that he would make a sorry card for the children (he felt unable to write a letter due to his lack of literary skills).

Upon leaving the victim shook hands with the young man and his parents and insisted that should they bump into each other again, they should smile and say hello. He also wished him luck for the future. As the Victim Liaison Officer escorted the victim out, he expressed his gratitude at being given the opportunity to meet the offender.

The case, from first meeting to the face-to-face meeting took 25 days (5 days over national standards for Referral Order Panel Meetings). The offender completed his contract over the following 9 months. The victim was given the option of being kept informed of his progress but declined this, saying he was satisfied with the outcome of the meeting and wanted to put the incident behind him.

Reflections

• The Victim Liaison Officer felt that the meeting was extremely successful. The victim left feeling that he had been listened to and that he had been given the opportunity to ask questions that had been troubling him and his family. He completed a feedback questionnaire in which he stated that he had found the process very helpful in getting over the incident. The offender had obviously been moved by the dialogue and went on to complete his order successfully.

- The success was assisted by the flexibility regarding the meeting taking place at a weekend etc. The victim would not have been able to afford to take time off work to attend during the week. In addition the panel members were trained to take a 'back seat' and let a dialogue develop between the parties, which assisted in both sides feeling ownership of the meeting and the outcome.

- The criminal justice system was saved the expense of this young man re-offending, as this meeting played a major part in the successful outcome of the order.

- The timescales set by the Youth Justice Board regarding Referral Order panel meetings being held within 20 days of the date at court can be problematic regarding victim involvement. Victims often want more time to consider their involvement and it would be helpful to have the time to do more preparation.

CASE 22 Arson in a small community

Two 15 year old boys set fire to a primary school, burning the building to the ground.

During the early hours a primary school at the heart of a village was burnt to the ground. The loss to such a small community was devastating. The building, equipment and records stretching back for almost a century had gone.

Shock soon turned to anger when news broke that 2 youths had been arrested and charged with arson.

The 2 youths, Greg and Damien, both aged 15 years, later appeared before the Crown Court, pleaded guilty to causing £2.5 million of damage to the school and were sentenced to a 2 year Supervision Order. Both sincerely regretted their foolish and reckless behaviour and, to their credit, expressed the need to do what they could to make amends to those affected by the fire.

During their supervision the case was referred to a victim/young offender mediation service that operates within the Youth Offending Team.

Mediation

The mediators, who work in pairs, arranged to meet with the Head Teacher of the school. During the meeting the implications of the boys' behaviour soon became apparent along with the harm and damage that had been caused to the school and community. The Head Teacher expressed the need, should a meeting take place with the 2 young offenders, that other representatives be involved as the staff, children, parents and the community were all 'victims' and had all been affected, in different ways, by the fire.

The mediators later visited Greg and Damien at their respective homes in the presence of their parents. They were both prepared to meet their 'victims' and do what they could to make amends.

A further meeting was arranged with the Head Teacher and also present was a member of staff, a parent whose child attended the school and representatives of the village and school's governing body. They all wanted to meet with the youths and their parents to explain how the fire had affected their lives.

3 months after the first meeting with the Head Teacher, the mediation between Greg, Damien and their victims took place. The meeting lasted nearly 3 hours. There was a short break and refreshments were available. The discussion was, at times, so intense that it was felt any adjournment would have lost the moment. A very frank, healthy and emotional exchange of information followed that resulted in the boys:

- Explaining what had happened
- Apologising for what they had done
- Answering questions about the incident
- Agreeing to write personal letters of apology to the Head Teacher
- Agreeing to do some reparation work for the benefit of the school and community
- Agreeing to write a joint letter for distribution to parents of children at the school, staff at the school and school Governors

- Agreeing to the joint letter being publicised in the local newspaper

The meeting was, at times, very sensitive and although confidentiality was, and will continue to be, respected, there was a need for information to be released publicly to inform the school and the community what actually happened. Greg and Damien agreed to write a joint letter for public distribution.

Letter of Apology

The letter they later wrote is as follows:

To the teachers, staff and children at the school, members of the local community and any other people affected by the fire at the school.

We set the wheelie bin on fire in the grounds of the school then left it to go back to where we were camping out. We left the bin because we thought it would burn out itself. We did not intentionally intend to set the school on fire but accept that our actions caused the fire at the school.

We now know how upsetting and how much work it has caused everyone at the school and in the village.

After the fire we were arrested by the Police and later charged. We then appeared at the Magistrates Court and were given a curfew from 9 pm to 7 am during which time we had to be with our parents. Then we went to Crown Court for trial. We both pleaded guilty and were sentenced to a 2 year supervision order. It all took a year and it was very scary for us and our parents were very upset.

We both feel better that the court hearings are over with and are trying hard to put right the damage and harm that has been done.

We later had a meeting with the Head Teacher and other people from the school and community to discuss what happened and to apologise personally.

We are both really sorry about it all and what we have done and will never do anything like this again.

All aspects of the agreement were completed in full. The above letter was published in the local newspaper. Under the supervision of a joiner, Greg and Damien made a wooden bench that was later presented to the Head Teacher for use in the school grounds.

"I feel I have owned up to my responsibility and tried to make things better. The meeting took the weight off my shoulders"

The outcome

Although a traumatic and emotional experience for all involved there was a strong sense of relief and closure voiced at the end of the meeting.

Feedback questionnaires returned from participants were very positive about the service they had received. 9 months following the mediation Greg and Damien were asked to reflect on the meeting and Damien said "I thought it was useful as I learnt what had happened to everyone and not just myself". Greg said "I feel I have owned up to my responsibility and tried to make things better. The meeting took the weight off my shoulders".

...they do deserve credit for having the gumption to say sorry in a regional newspaper that circulates in the village.

Neither of the boys has re-offended.

The editor of a regional newspaper that featured the story wrote:

'It is tempting to say to the two boys who have publicly apologised for burning down [the village school] 18 months ago that it's a bit late now. But they do deserve credit for having the gumption to say sorry in a regional newspaper that circulates in the village. The two secondary school pupils who set fire to a wheelie bin with disastrous consequences also say they are trying hard to put right the harm and damage caused. The signs are that some good is emerging from this episode – and that is due in no small measure to the enlightened way in which these young offenders have been dealt with by their own community, not least by the school Head Teacher herself.'

Reflections

- Apart from the benefits to all concerned through mediation the restorative approach provided meaningful activity for the boys during which they developed their interpersonal skills and confidence, and learnt new skills during the manufacture of the bench.

- No hindrance was experienced other than the issue of protecting the identity of the young boys. The protection of their identity is paramount and unlawful to do otherwise. Working with them in a restorative way was challenging due to the high profile of the case, the fact that the community knew who they were and what they had done, together with the attraction of media attention.

CASE 23 Indecent assault involving young people with learning difficulties

A 13 year old boy indecently assaulted a 16 year old girl. Both the victim and offender had learning difficulties.

Deano was a well-built, strong 13 year-old boy with learning difficulties and severe emotional and behavioural difficulties. He attended a day school which could cater for his special needs. He was easily led by older pupils and, as he had matured, this had resulted in Deano often being involved in trouble. He lived with his mother in a large village community and they owned a block of land on which they kept a few horses. The land adjoined open countryside surrounding the village, which the local teenagers found useful as their secret play area.

The offence

One autumn evening Deano and a 17 year-old male, Adrian, were feeding the horses and Adrian was boasting about his prowess with girls. Deano had never had a girlfriend and Adrian mocked him for his innocence. A little later, two 16 year-old female school friends (both with learning difficulties) arrived. One of the girls, Jane, was a regular visitor as she often came to feed the horses. Adrian incited and encouraged Deano to make a pass at Jane. Jane was embarrassed and didn't know what to do. Her friend quickly went home but, as Jane tried to leave, Deano caught her and dragged her into undergrowth where he clumsily, indecently assaulted her.

The outcome

The investigation was prolonged because of Jane's fear of naming the offender. Finally, 3 months later, the Youth Offending Service referred the case, at Pre-Sentence Report stage. There was concern for the victim and her family and, also, Deano was not accepting full responsibility for the offence. The mediator was able to challenge Deano during an assessment in the presence of his Mother, Tricia. Deano eventually acknowledged what he had done.

Following telephone contact with Jane's mother, Gail, a visit to the family home was arranged at a time when Gail would be alone. Gail explained that her whole family had been devastated by the offence and she was trying to maintain some sense of normality and prevent repercussions. Jane had become withdrawn and hardly spoke to her mother any more. Gail was very concerned about her emotional health. She and her husband had separated 18 months ago and he lived with his partner 10 miles away. When he was told of the offence he was livid and Gail was having great difficulty in restraining him from taking vengeance on Deano. Their 21 year old son was working away from home and he had not been informed of the offence as there was concern that he might over-react. Gail had lost 2 stones in weight and felt she couldn't speak to anyone about what had happened.

Deano's first appearance in Court resulted in his receiving a 2 year Supervision Order and an entry on the Sex Offender Register. During her next visit to the victim's mother, the mediator explained what the order would entail. She discovered that Jane was back at school and had put the incident behind her and her father had calmed down, but Gail was no better. The mediator then visited Deano's mother and discovered that she was also having difficulties coming to terms with what had happened.

During a period of indirect mediation, both mothers decided that a mediation meeting could prove useful. The meeting was held one morning when the children were at school.

During a period of indirect mediation, both mothers decided that a mediation meeting could prove useful. The meeting was held one morning when the children were at school. The 2 women came from long-established village families and had known one another all their lives. They had simultaneously attended the village primary school, in consecutive year groups. Tricia was highly embarrassed by her son's behaviour and wanted Gail to know that in no way did she condone it. She was eager to apologise to her and find out how Jane was feeling. Gail was relieved to be able to speak about it at last because they had both been avoiding one another in the village.

They talked kindly with one another for a long time, supported by many cups of tea, and the meeting was often emotional. They agreed on a plan that would help to protect both their children but also allow them freedom to play and socialise in the village. They also wanted to be able to get feedback from each other as to how their plan was working, but were worried that telephone calls may be accessed by other members of the family. The mediator agreed to be the go-between for them.

> "They agreed on a plan that would help to protect both their children but also allow them freedom to play and socialise in the village."

The meeting had been cathartic for both women and their plan worked excellently. The mediator initially telephoned on a weekly basis and over a period of 3 months gradually reduced it to once a month.

Mediation would not have been a suitable option for the victim and offender, but on this occasion, it was appropriate for the 2 mothers and they each benefited from it. The monitoring of the situation by the parents meant that the young people could each quickly resume their leisure pastimes and put the incident behind them.

Within a short space of time Gail had re-gained weight. She felt that closure on the matter had been achieved.

> Mediation would not have been a suitable option for the victim and offender, but on this occasion, it was appropriate for the 2 mothers and they each benefited from it.

Tricia was proud that she had been able to help Gail recover from the trauma and her sense of self-respect was restored, without minimising her son's actions.

The 2 mothers were able to speak to one another again instead of avoiding each other.

Reflections

- Accurate assessment is the key to all work with offenders, and assessing young people with emotional and behavioural difficulties is particularly difficult. Often, a Pre-Sentence Report (PSR) author will become the Supervising Officer of the young person, following sentence. Thus, during the assessment process, there is a need to engage with the young person and also challenge their views and attitudes. Sometimes this seems to be contradictory and in this case the boy (who had pleaded guilty) was, nevertheless, refusing to accept or discuss the offence. The PSR author asked the Restorative Justice Worker to do a challenging assessment to help the young person to accept responsibility for the offence. This was successful in this case and helped the court to deliver a correct sentence and the boy to begin his order positively.

- The restorative intervention certainly restored Gail to better physical and emotional health and, perhaps saved money for the Health Service.
- If there had been no restorative intervention, the growing animosity in the village could (and probably would) have resulted in further incidents. It could be argued that the restorative justice intervention prevented an escalation of the dispute.

CASE 24   Attempted robbery of an elderly shopkeeper

Two 15 year old boys attempted to rob a local corner shop, threatening and frightening the elderly shopkeeper.

Naseem and Ryan had become friends through attending the same school. The pair had discussed ways of making money after Ryan had told Naseem of his bleak home situation. His father had been imprisoned after trying to kill his mother and the family home was having to be sold. Ryan was acutely aware of his mother's difficult financial situation and felt responsible for her. In his misguided attempt to 'help', the two boys hatched a plan to rob a shop. Although initially Naseem was reluctant to become involved he eventually agreed to assist his friend.

The offence

One summer's evening, 15 year old Naseem and Ryan entered a local corner store after ensuring that there were no other customers present. They spent some time looking around before they plucking up the courage to approach the elderly shopkeeper Mr Banerjee. They had gone in to the shop with the intention of robbing the shopkeeper and had gone equipped to do so. Naseem had a knife hidden up his sleeve and Ryan had an imitation gun hidden down the front of his trousers. They approached the counter and Naseem demanded that Mr Banerjee hand over the contents of the till, holding the knife in his left hand as he did so.

Mr Banerjee refused their request and picked up the telephone to call the police. At this both boys ran out of the shop empty handed. They were arrested shortly afterwards for attempted robbery after being caught in a nearby underpass where they were changing into different clothing. The knife and clothing were found in a rucksack they had with them.

The shopkeeper was extremely shocked after the incident and described feeling frightened and concerned for his safety.

The decision to meet

Prior to the boys being sentenced by the court, a Police Officer who was attached to the Youth Offending Team and experienced in Restorative Conferencing visited Mr Banerjee at his home. The possibility of Direct Reparation between Mr Banerjee and the two youths was explored and discussed. Mr Banerjee stated that he would be more than happy to participate in a Restorative Conference and would welcome the chance to hear from the boys themselves the reasons for their actions.

Neither of the youths had ever offended before and the offence was therefore was totally out of character for both of them. Their respective families were extremely distressed when they learned of their sons' behaviour. Both youths expressed their shame and remorse for their actions and vowed never to offend again. Naseem and Ryan also said they would appreciate the opportunity to meet with the victim.

Because the victim had voluntarily expressed a desire to meet with the two young men concerned and they themselves had said that they wanted to apologise to him in person, it was written into the Pre-Sentence Report that this would happen. As a result, the court made it a requirement of the

Supervision Order.

All parties were subsequently contacted again and the Restorative Conferencing process explained in detail. A venue was booked for the conference to take place in neutral surroundings 4 days before Christmas. Both Ryan and Naseem expressed the wish to face Mr Banerjee alone without either of their parents being present, but were naturally nervous about how the process would evolve.

The meeting

The boys were already seated when Mr Banerjee walked in. He immediately shook their hands, which clearly put them at ease. The Youth Offending Team Police Officer then ran the conference in a structured manner, allowing each person the time and space to talk about what had happened. Mr Banerjee explained to the boys about how their actions had affected him and the boys expressed their remorse at the distress they had caused.

At the conclusion of the conference Mr Banerjee told the boys how impressed he had been by their willingness to meet him. He invited both the boys to visit him in the shop with their Mothers to "have a cup of tea with him".

Before leaving he handed each boy a £10 note and wished them a very "Happy Christmas!" Both Naseem and Ryan thanked Mr Banerjee profusely and appeared genuinely moved by his generosity. Ryan beamed and said "at least I'll be able to buy my mum a Christmas present now".

This Restorative Conference was one of the most moving and successful that the facilitator had ever witnessed. The process taught Ryan and Naseem so much about the kindness and forgiveness of the victim even though they had offended against him. Through the process they both gained a valuable insight in to the victim's perspective.

At the conclusion of the conference Mr Banerjee told the boys how impressed he had been by their willingness to meet him. He invited both the boys to visit him in the shop with their mothers to "have a cup of tea with him".

Reflections

- The success of this case was due to all parties being well prepared as to what the conference would entail. In choosing a venue that was in a neutral location and had a calm, relaxed atmosphere, none of the parties felt threatened.

CASE 25 Endangering persons using railways: a sack of manure

Three teenage boys hung a sack of manure from a bridge. When the train hit it, it obstructed the drivers vision and caused distress to passengers.

The offence

3 teenagers hung a sack of manure from a railway bridge to see what would happen when a train went past and hit it. The manure partially obstructed the drivers vision, and caused distress to the passengers who were unaware of what the substance soiling the train was.

"This is not about punishment, it is about opening their eyes...and inviting them back."

The boys received Reparation Orders for the offence of 'endangering persons using railways'. It was agreed that the boys would assist with the cleaning of trains.

The reparation

The trains were cleaned at night, and the boys were given a warm welcome from the cleaning team. Their supervisor insisted that they were all co-workers for the night. "This is not about punishment" he said, showing an instinctive grasp of reparation, "it is about opening their eyes...and inviting them back."

The boys discovered that joining the nightshift is tough. However, they rose to the challenge and got stuck in, clearing rubbish, wiping tables, mopping floors and scrubbing the toilets of 6 trains, paying back to the train operator with cloths, brushes, mops, and their own sweat. "It has to be done" said one of the boys, all of whom agreed that reparation was the best way to make amends for their offence.

The hardest thing for the boys was the impact upon their families – made worse by local newspapers falsely suggesting that bricks were thrown at the train. After the reparation, the boys hoped that they could put the offence behind them, and one said, "I'm just glad it's over".

Reflections

• The Reparation Supervisor asked the question 'Was the harm repaired?'. The offenders and those from the railway company agreed that it had been.

• When setting up the reparation, the Reparation Supervisor spoke to railway staff from many different companies – all of whom expressed appreciation of the restorative approach.

• Reparation succeeded because the reparation was a perfect match for the offence, enabling everyone to make perfect sense of what it was about, and giving the boys the opportunity to 'do sorry', to pay back with their own efforts in order to move on. In the process they helped build bridges with rail staff who may have had negative stereotypes of young people who offend against the railways.

• There were no particular welfare issues for these three boys, and by concentrating solely on practical reparation for their cases, money may have been saved in the long run.

• Laws and guidelines made this creative and appropriate response possible within the context of existing legislation.

CASE 26 **Criminal damage: burnt bridges?**

*A 15 year old boy sawed pieces of wood off
a bridge and built a fire which caused
£2,500 worth of damage.*

At Christmas 2001, 15 year old Robin was out with a group of friends, at their usual meeting place – a den in a hollowed out thorn bush. They had a set of tools including a saw, an axe, a hammer and nails. During the evening, Robin had an argument with a friend and ran off with the saw.

He ran and sat by a bridge nearby, getting very cold. He decided to saw bits of wood off the bridge to build a fire to keep warm. He sat by the fire for about an hour while he calmed down, and then went home. A witness called the Police and Robin was arrested. As he had previously received a Final Warning, the matter was referred to Court.

Robin came to the Youth Offending Team after receiving a 3 month Action Plan Order for a Criminal Damage offence. He was a bright young man who was studying for his GCSE's and was on target to obtain high grades. Robin's parents were extremely distressed by his involvement in the incident and talked openly about their shame and embarrassment, particularly having to go to Court, and being made subject to a Parental Bindover.

Whilst preparing the Pre-Sentence Report, contact was made with the local council who owned the bridge. They agreed that it would be appropriate for a representative of the local council to meet with Robin in a Restorative Justice Conference, to help him understand the consequences of his actions and to give him an opportunity to repair some of the harm he caused.

Robin wanted to meet with the representative, as he wanted to apologise for what he had done. His parents were keen for the meeting to take place so that Robin could gain a better understanding of the impact of his behaviour on other people.

The mediators met with Robin and his mother Betty on 2 occasions prior to the meeting to ensure they understood the process and to answer any questions they might have. Robin decided that he only wanted Betty to be present at the meeting, as he was concerned that his father had been unwell and he did not want to make things worse for him. His parents agreed with this decision.

The mediators also met with Paul, the council representative who was going to attend the meeting, to explain the process to him. This was to ensure that the process was as safe as possible for everyone involved. Paul informed the mediators that he had some photographs of the damage, which totalled £2,500, and suggested he show them to Robin and his mother at the meeting. Paul also agreed to liaise with the farmer involved, to obtain his views on the matter.

The meeting

The meeting took place at the Youth Offending Team office as this was felt to be a safe, neutral environment. Paul arrived 10 minutes before Robin and his Mother, to avoid any difficult first meetings on the doorstep. When Robin and his Mother arrived, Paul immediately shook Robin's hand and spoke to Betty, who appeared very nervous.

After introductions, the mediator asked Robin to tell those people present, exactly what had happened on the evening. Despite being nervous,

What she read was powerful and shocked everyone, especially Robin, who fought hard not to cry.

Robin was able to explain fully what had happened and to demonstrate a limited understanding of the effects on others. Paul then explained to the meeting how he first found out about the damage to the bridge, what effect the incident had on others, including the local farmer whose cattle were grazing in the field and escaped as a result of the damage. He showed the photographs to the meeting. Betty was visibly shocked and upset when she saw the extent of the damage, as was Robin.

Betty was then asked to say how she felt about the matter. She produced 2 pieces of paper that she and Robin's father had prepared together, which she asked to read out. What she read was powerful and shocked everyone, especially Robin, who fought hard not to cry. It was clear that Betty's words were genuine and that Robin had previously had no idea of the hurt and upset he had caused his parents. Robin's parents were very committed to helping him make positive changes in his life and saw the meeting as a way of telling him how they felt.

Robin apologised to Paul for what he had done, and Paul agreed to pass this on to his Manager and colleagues. However Robin offered to write to them, and the Leader of the Council, expressing his remorse. Robin's mother suggested that he should also write to the farmer, whose cattle had escaped as a result of the damage. These letters were subsequently written and sent to the relevant people.

Robin apologised to his mother in the meeting, something which (he admitted later), was harder than doing so to the victim.

At the conclusion of the meeting, Paul and Robin struck up a conversation about motorbikes. Paul was able to tell him where there are approved, organised sites for him to take part in 'off road motorcycling'. Paul also told Robin that he hoped he would see him in the future using the countryside facilities in a positive way.

Post meeting

Some months later, Robin and Paul were featured in *Youth Justice Board News*, as an example of the positive benefits of Restorative Justice. By this time, Robin had finished working with the Youth Offending Team and was making good progress in his life, studying hard for his GCSEs and working part-time to repay his parents for the fine they received. There had been no further offending and it was hoped that Robin's brief contact with the criminal justice system was over. Nonetheless, he wanted to share his story with others – he and his parents felt that this may help other offenders and victims in the future, and in turn reduce offending by young people.

Reflections

- The success of this piece of work was largely due to the commitment of Robin, his family and Paul. All parties wanted a positive outcome and were prepared to do whatever was necessary to achieve this. Within the local area there is a strong commitment from all agencies working with young people to use restorative justice approaches to achieve positive outcomes for victims and offenders, and those close to them.
- Despite being a representative of a 'corporate' victim, Paul took a

personal interest in the case and in Robin's future. Robin's parents' commitment to and understanding of the process also made the experience more meaningful for him.

CASE 27 **Assault on a former friend**

A 15 year old boy assaulted a former friend
after being excluded from school.

15 year old Darren and Josh attended the same large comprehensive school. Darren was not an academic boy, and was frequently in trouble whilst Josh came from a more privileged background and achieved well academically. Despite their differences, the two boys became good friends who were popular with their peers.

However, a disagreement between the boys led to Darren being excluded (again) from school. Darren felt unfairly treated and waited for Josh outside school one day. Darren beat Josh so seriously that he needed treatment in Accident and Emergency. Darren found himself permanently excluded from school, appeared in Court and received a 3 month Action Plan Order.

Back at school other boys were taking sides and there was quite clearly an incident waiting to happen. What was at an early stage bravado and empty threats could easily have turned into something worse.

The victim's story

It was at this stage that the Victim Liaison Officers from the Youth Offending Team (both trained mediators) became involved. They arranged to visit Josh and his dad to offer information and to talk through the options open to them. Both were aware of, and unhappy about, the underlying tension. Josh's dad was particularly worried that his son might be goaded to retaliate physically, which could lead to a criminal record. They agreed that some form of mediation could be useful, but that it was something for the boys themselves to participate in, rather than the parents, who did not know one another.

The offender's story

When Darren was visited, he was less articulate, but clearly shared similar worries to those of Josh and his dad. Darren and his dad were also aware that the feelings of their friends could escalate into another incident. Darren felt that his record would mean that he would have to shoulder the blame whatever happened. On the other hand, he no longer wanted to apologise as he felt that Josh and his friends had been aggravating the situation and making threats.

The focus of the discussion changed. Darren's dad felt that a meeting between the boys could establish ground rules for future behaviour and take the sting out of neighbourhood rumours. He also felt that showing each boy the other's true state of mind would be useful and Darren agreed.

Some time elapsed whilst Josh was on holiday, but he agreed to a meeting on the terms suggested by both parties on his return.

The meeting

The meeting took place in a Community Centre half way between the homes of each boy. The boys needed little encouragement to talk frankly about the incident and its outcome and their underlying concern for each other shone through. Josh admitted that he had been goading Darren before the fight and showed sorrow and concern that Darren could now not complete his education but was instead in a 'dead end job'. Darren said he enjoyed having wages and anyway, because of costs and compensation, he was in a position to pay his debts himself. Both boys were worried about the possibility of further 'aggro' from their friends. They agreed that they could do a lot to minimise risk by assuring everyone that the whole incident was now closed. They talked amicably for some

The boys needed little encouragement to talk frankly about the incident and its outcome and their underlying concern for each other shone through.

minutes about their plans for the future and then drew up an agreement.

The agreement

Because Darren and Josh had talked frankly they could put the past behind them and if they met they would both be able to say 'hello'. Darren apologised for what had happened and Josh apologised for aggravating the situation. They both left the meeting smiling.

The outcome

About a month after the meeting, the Victim Liaison Officers did their formal follow up work. This follow up is designed to check that the work has been done professionally, and that there are no issues left over that need addressing. Josh and his dad were most enthusiastic and Josh's dad in particular felt this kind of work was a "really worthwhile use of public money".

Josh's dad in particular felt this kind of work was a "really worthwhile use of public money"

Darren demonstrated the success of the meeting by not coming to the attention of the Youth Offending Team again once his order was completed.

Reflections

- The support of the dads of both boys helped this case reach a successful outcome. Both parties recognised that there were issues that could not easily be addressed in any other way (i.e. the worries about possible repercussions from the boys or their friends), and both boys did not want to leave things unresolved.
- The support of those colleagues within the team who were responsible for Darren's Order assisted in the success of the work.
- It is possible that further offending behaviour was prevented by the meeting.

CASE 28 Assault with actual bodily harm: a victim living in fear

A 15 year old boy assaulted a 17 year old boy, causing Actual Bodily Harm. The victim was terrified of what would happen if he saw the offender locally.

15 year old Tom was a very tall, stocky and strong boy. He was convicted of the assault (with Actual Bodily Harm) of another boy who, although older, was much slighter in build.

The assault happened after an argument about some girls and Tom was given a 20 hour Action Plan Order and a referral to the victim-offender mediation service.

2 trained mediators met with Tom and discussed the possibilities of mediation between himself and the victim. The mediators had to work hard to get Tom interested and involved, yet with the knowledge that this work had to be victim led.

The victim's story

The mediators then met the victim, Shaun, who was 17 years old. Shaun's entire family was present at the meeting and it was clear that they had all been devastated by the offence and were still living in great fear and anxiety.

Shaun's mum and dad were especially concerned because since the offence there had been a number of times when Shaun bumped into Tom in the town centre. Verbal threats had been made towards him along with a 'cut throat' sign. This terrified the whole family and left them concerned about what the future might bring. The mediators spent a lot of time listening to the family, as each individually expressed their fears and concerns.

The first priority, as mediators, was to be honest and help the family see that this case was reliant on Tom being willing to hear from the victims. It was important the family realised that the mediators did not have a miracle

"It was clear that they had all been devastated by the offence and were still living in great fear and anxiety."

cure to offer. Through discussion it was agreed that Tom should not know everybody's intimate concerns in case this led to further offences. Also, the family did not want Tom to become empowered by knowledge of personal details.

It was agreed that what all the family wanted, including Shaun, was some assurance that he would be left alone in the future. The mediators agreed to go back to Tom and tell him a little of the family's concern. Tom would be asked to think about this and perhaps write something down about his future intentions towards Shaun.

The offender's story

The mediators then met with Tom and talked about the offence. Tom appeared to imply that he was laughing at the victim because Shaun was older than him. Tom was asked if he was frightened of anything. His first reply was, 'No!' However, on further investigation he admitted that he was frightened of spiders. The mediators asked him if there was any difference between the fear of spiders and the fear of an individual. After working with Tom for some time the mediators asked what his

The mediators asked him if there was any difference between the fear of spiders and the fear of an individual.

intention would be if he were to bump into the Shaun again. (They did not mention that they knew that this had already happened). Tom said that it was all over now and he was 'not going to get him'. It was suggested that he might communicate his feelings towards Tom in some way – provided that he meant it.

The outcome

Tom did this – he wrote a letter to Shaun with the agreement that the mediators would pass it on. The mediators hoped that this would at least 'break the ice' between the 2 boys.

However, one mediator fell ill and it was not possible to meet Shaun and his family for another 10 days. When they eventually met again, as they entered Shaun's front room they got a surprise. The whole atmosphere was completely different. Shaun and his family explained to the mediators that since their last meeting, Shaun was riding his bike into the town centre and was flagged down by Tom and his friends. Tom's friends shouted, 'Go on, hit him, hit him!' To the amazement of Shaun, Tom turned around to his mates and said, 'No, I won't!' He put out his hand to shake hands and said, 'It's all forgotten.' Shaun and his family felt excited that this had happened. They were amazed.

Reflections

- Mediators needed to bring a word of caution to Shaun's family about discussing their concerns with others outside, as 'what goes around, comes around'. However it was important for them to know that they indirectly achieved a successful outcome. It was also felt important that Tom and Shaun knew they had brought about the changes themselves.
- When Tom was asked what he thought of his involvement, he replied that if he had not been involved with the mediation process he did not know what would have happened if he ever saw the Shaun in the street. Tom's mum was pleased because she thought her son might have snapped in anger at Shaun.
- The process showed Tom that he had sorted something out himself in a non-violent way.

CASE 29 Criminal damage to a community centre

A 15 year old boy smashed the windows of a Community Centre whilst under the influence of alcohol.

John was a slim built 15 year old schoolboy. He was the youngest of three, having two older sisters. His mother – a single parent – was supportive of

John, but expressed embarrassment and disappointment following John's offence.

John's school attendance had been poor and he was currently working to a reduced timetable with the Student Support Service. John had no previous offending history.

One evening John had been drinking strong lager with some friends in a local park. John described himself as being 'quite drunk' by the time he and his friends left the park and walked towards the local Community Centre.

John saw an empty beer crate near to the Community Centre. He picked the crate up and threw it towards one of the Community Centre windows, smashing it. John then staggered away with his friends.

Arrest

A short time later, the Police (as a result of information received by local residents, who could positively identify him) arrested John.

John fully admitted the offence and could offer no explanation as to why he had done it, other than the fact that he was very drunk.

John was charged with Criminal Damage, and received an 18 hour Reparation Order from the Court.

The Youth Offending Team worker responsible for supervising John with his reparation hours began with a session of leaflet dropping for the local YWCA.

Apology

During this time they talked about his offence, and John asked the worker whether it would be possible to apologise face-to-face to the Community Centre Manager instead of, or as well as, a letter of apology.

The worker then contacted the Restorative Justice Worker in the Youth Offending Team.

John was visited at home with the reparation worker. John's mum was also present.

John expressed regret and remorse for his actions and repeated his wish to apologise to the Community Centre Manager. John's mother was supportive of her son's wishes and agreed to be present should such a meeting take place.

Contact was made with Lucy, the Community Centre Manager and Youth Worker. Lucy agreed to a meeting after the principles of Restorative Justice had been explained to her.

It was felt that both parties would benefit from a Restorative Conference.

The meeting was arranged for a morning the following week in the main hall of the Community Centre. Approximately 2 hours had been spent with each participant and half an hour with John's mum.

At the meeting Lucy seemed composed and focused. John, and particularly his mother, Jackie, appeared nervous. The Youth Offending Service Reparation Worker was present with the permission of all parties.

After introductions, and an explanation about the purpose of the meeting, it was explained that the conference was the result of a direct request from John, and he was invited to give his account of events leading up to, during, and after the offence.

During this explanation, John took full responsibility for his actions, expressed appropriate remorse and ended with a sincere apology.

Lucy, clearly moved, thanked John for showing the courage to participate in the conference, and accepted his apology. Lucy then went on to explain the consequences of John's offence. She began by describing the inconvenience of being called out late at night by the Police, and having to wait until the building had been secured. Lucy then talked about the financial impact and the effect on insurance premiums etc, and also the time spent clearing broken glass inside the Centre. At this point Lucy pointed out that the Community Centre was a focal point for all members of the community (which included John) to come together and to enjoy leisure activities. This centre was very much a part of John and his family's community.

It was then the turn of John's mother, who began by apologising to Lucy for her son's behaviour. She gave an emotional account of her feelings of embarrassment and shame when the Police came to her house in the early hours of the morning to tell her that John had been arrested.

She described the inconvenience

"She gave an emotional account of her feelings of embarrassment and shame when the Police came to her house in the early hours of the morning to tell her that John had been arrested."

caused trying to arrange a babysitter for her baby niece whom she was currently caring for. She told the conference that she felt as though she had done something wrong herself whilst acting as an appropriate adult during her son's interview at the Police Station. She ended her contribution by adding that although she had experienced this shame, she now felt proud that John had been courageous enough to face up to his actions and was trying to repair some of the harm caused.

Reparation

Lucy was asked if there was any direct reparation work that John could do in the Community Centre to complete his reparation hours. Lucy said that the shrub area to the side of the Community Centre was in need of tidying and John agreed to do this.

The majority of John's remaining hours were completed at the Community Centre. Following one of these sessions the Reparation Worker was taking John home when they witnessed another offence taking place. John told the worker the name of the main perpetrator (someone he knew from school), and asked that this information be passed to the police. John has not re-offended.

Reflections

• The conference was successful in that all parties expressed satisfaction during de-brief.
• The detailed preparation of the parties and their willingness to participate were major factors in the successful outcome of this case.
• The restorative approach may have saved the criminal justice system time, money and work as John has not re-offended.
• Existing laws and guidelines did not make it difficult to work in a restorative way.

CASE 30 Intent to supply drugs and burglary: a father and son mediation

A mediation was set up for a father and son following the son's criminal behaviour.

Roger was an unemployed 17 year old living with his father Sid. Roger was one of a group of young men who dealt drugs and committed burglary in order to make money. His father felt victimised by Roger's actions, because of police raids, neighbours' disapproval and lack of trust in the home. Sid felt he was distanced from Roger because he was more than 40 years older than his son, because he was a recovering alcoholic, and because he was often blamed for the unexplained disappearance of his wife, Roger's mother.

Roger was given a Community Service Order and referred to the Mediation Service (in November) by his Youth Offending Team (Yot) worker. We saw him first after a regular Yot appointment. We explained that mediation is a voluntary process, and he agreed that we should visit his father. Roger felt that his father played 'mind games' with him, and that there were questions about his mother that he wanted to ask Sid. Roger also expressed the wish to stay with his father and 'do whatever he wants'.

We visited Sid in his home. He explained his own difficulties in emotional terms. His house was an important haven. Roger was threatening that by bringing his troubles home. Most of all Sid was concerned that he would slip back into alcoholism and lose everything. He had coped best when Roger had been taken into care in previous years. One concern that Sid also had was that Roger was also showing signs of an addictive personality, and so he had taken him to an Alcoholics Anonymous (AA) meeting.

The first joint meeting (December) was between the two of them with two mediators. We followed mediation methods, but not any prescribed format. We tried to establish an agenda of issues. Roger would not speak at first. Sid spoke about his own perspective and concerns. We empathised through summarising, highlighting positives such as 'I love my son, but can't cope with things he does' and praising them for attending.

Roger gave us permission to say that he wanted to raise issues about living at home and house rules. We wrote them up on the flip chart, and tried to start negotiating about if/when friends could visit, but Sid stormed out at this point. We spoke with him in a separate room, but he insisted he was not going to allow any changes to his

"We empathised through summarising, highlighting positives such as 'I love my son, but can't cope with things he does' and praising them for attending."

rules. He said he wanted to leave and offered money for a taxi for Roger to get home. I asked how he thought Roger would feel about that and he told me I was 'laying guilt' on him. He left very upset by my question. Roger had had enough too, but agreed to see us again. On reflection this had been a transforming moment in the mediation, as Sid began to think of Roger as his responsibility, and we began to understand Sid's needs too.

We were relieved that we were able to arrange further visits (January) to their home. First we saw Sid. He was calmer, and had had support from his AA mentor. We explained that we would not ask him to do something he could not cope with, and he agreed to continue with mediation. Roger's difficulties had continued involving the police and Sid thought the court wanted to revisit Roger's sentence. When we met Roger he spoke passionately that he wanted answers to big questions about his mother, and told us that he was being breached for non-compliance with his Community Service Order.

The second joint meeting (February) was mainly backward looking, going over Roger's childhood and searching for answers to questions. Sid

It felt cathartic but we were aware we are not trained as counsellors.

answered with candour, and in a supportive way. Roger was clear about what he wanted to know, and voiced the most difficult question about Sid's involvement. Mediators heard the exchange but took no part except providing a safe, calm environment. In some ways we felt frustrated by not being able to address practical issues. It felt cathartic but we were aware we are not trained as

counsellors. Sid agreed to one of Roger's friends being involved in finding more information from other members of the family. This was a step

---

forward for them both. Sid accepted one of Roger's friends and trusted Roger. We agreed to arrange another joint meeting.

At this point a surprise letter arrived from Roger's Solicitor in relation to the breach hearing in court. Roger's Solicitor wrote asking for information about mediation, what had happened and what had been agreed. We asked Sid and Roger for permission to tell the solicitor that mediation was in progress, that they had attended all their appointments with us, and that a third meeting was planned. We were not willing to release confidential details. As a result of the Solicitor's report to the court, which included his own observations of the improving relationship between father and son, the community sentence was not changed to a custodial one. The Judge expressed his appreciation of the involvement of the mediation service.

In preparation for the third meeting (April) we decided we did not want to create dependency. We were not able to meet Roger's possible needs for drug, bereavement, or career counselling, though, in liaising with the Yot, we could make sure he knew how to contact them. We could not commit service resources or Yot funding to a continued series of meetings. Fortunately the relationship was improving and confidence was growing in their own abilities to talk and trust each other. They were both pleased with the court decision. The meeting ended with agreement that father and son would work together to help Roger find work. They agreed to start afresh each day if there had been failure before, and to limit the time spent on job-hunting each day. Other issues were not addressed but both Sid and Roger accepted that it would be the last meeting. Both indicated that they were pleased with their own progress and the help of the Mediation Service.

Reflections

- We judged success by feedback from clients, Solicitor, Judge and each other. It 'felt right'.
- This mediation, offered to Roger whilst he was undertaking a Community Service Order, provided an opportunity to work on the issues that simultaneously threatened Roger's accommodation and his relationship with his father.
- The main issue was communication between father and son; mediation was ideal for this.
- This mediation saved the cost of custodial sentence, and saved the

criminal justice time, using over 40 hours of mediator time over 5 months. It also prevented Roger having to leave home.

* The mediation service were not expecting the Solicitor enquiry and found the questioning from Solicitors inappropriate and unhelpful. We did not want to lose the trust we had developed with both Roger and Sid, and had maintained that we were not part of the Criminal Justice system.

CASE 31   Criminal damage after a row with girlfriend

A young man smashed an office window causing
fear and distress to the office workers inside.

A young man was out with his girlfriend in town and they had a major row. Eventually they parted ways but as he walked along the young man got angrier and angrier.

The young man felt absolutely consumed by his anger and as a way of releasing it, picked up debris lying in the street and launched it at a nearby office block. As he threw the bricks and stones he swore and shouted the vile names he was now associating with his girlfriend.

Inside the building were female office workers. Most were on the first floor but one woman was on the ground floor doing photocopying. She suffered the full impact of the attack. Suddenly the windows came crashing through. There was glass showering around her and she heard shouting and swearing. She didn't know what had happened and was terrified. All sorts of thoughts went through her head – Were they the target of terrorists or criminals, and was she in immediate danger?

Upstairs the other workers were also bewildered and shocked.

The young man's destructive spree only lasted about 5 minutes but it left the workers shaken and frightened. In addition, the office routine was disrupted for days whilst the windows were boarded and re-glazed, insurance claims were completed and the police conducted interviews.

Mediation

After his outburst, the young man was filled with remorse and gave himself up to the Police. The Court sentenced him to probation and his Probation Officer referred him for victim-offender mediation.

The mediators met with the young man and explored with him how he felt about the offence and whether he was willing to meet with the victims if they so wished. They felt that he was genuine in his desire to make amends and that it would be safe to contact the victims.

The office workers were pleased to meet with the mediators and tell them what had happened. The mediators heard that they had been very frightened and the woman downstairs in particular, had had to have time off work because she was so traumatised by what had happened. They ascertained that the office workers had a need to understand why this had happened – to know what the offender was like. It felt to them that he was a violent and dangerous criminal and they needed reassurance that this was a one-off and wouldn't happen again.

The mediators asked if they would nominate someone to meet with the offender face-to-face. At first they said not the woman who had been photocopying as she had already suffered more than the others. However the mediators pointed out that she probably was the one who was most in need of the healing that mediation can bring.

> *"It felt to them that he was a violent and dangerous criminal and they needed reassurance that this was a one-off and wouldn't happen again."*

It was agreed therefore that she would be the one to meet with the offender.

The meeting

The mediation took place on neutral territory at the mediation offices. Ground rules were agreed and then both the victim and the offender were given time to say what had happened and how they felt. The offender said how sorry he was. The victim asked him why he had done it. At the end of the meeting the victim said she was willing to accept the apology. It was agreed that she would relate to the rest of the staff what had happened.

Reflections

- Both the victim and offender said the mediation had helped them put the incident behind them. Both said that they felt better and both said they would recommend mediation to other victims and offenders.

CASE 32   Assault on a police officer by young woman under the influence of alcohol

A police officer was assaulted by a 17 year old whilst trying to dress her in the cell as she was under the influence of alcohol.

A case was referred in which a 17 year old female, Andrea, had assaulted a Police Officer whilst in custody on another matter. Andrea, who was placed on a Reparation Order, expressed remorse to her Youth Offending Team Officer who then referred the case.

The offender's story

The mediators visited Andrea before any contact with the victim. This was done to assess her suitability and willingness to participate in mediation. Andrea said that she did feel sorry about the assault and believed that it would not have happened had she not been influenced by alcohol. She also expressed her fear that her drink had been interfered with that evening. She decided to meet the Police Officer face-to-face if the Police Officer agreed.

The victim's story

The mediators then visited the Police Officer. She said that she felt especially aggrieved by the assault as when it occurred she had actually been trying to help Andrea. Apparently Andrea, having been under the influence of alcohol and, possibly drugs, had begun to undress herself in the Police cell. The Police Officer said that she was a mother of daughters around Andrea's age and she felt upset seeing her in the state she was in. She said that she only wanted to cover her up and protect her dignity. When she attempted to do this, Andrea lashed out, kicking and punching her. The Police Officer was left with severe bruising and soreness. She said that she wanted to meet Andrea to find out more about her and understand 'what had happened to bring her to this'.

The meeting

As both the victim and the offender were assessed as suitable and agreed, a face-to-face mediation was arranged. The ground rules were read and agreed to and the Police Officer was given the opportunity to speak first. She began by saying that on the night of the assault she had had only been trying to help Andrea. However, she then began to ask several questions about what kind of person Andrea was. At this point, Andrea was visibly angry and became very quiet and defensive.

Overcoming problems

The mediation began to lose momentum and a break was called. One mediator went with Andrea and asked her how she was feeling. Andrea said that she felt as though she was being cross-examined and looked down upon. The mediator explained that it was all right to feel what she was feeling and that maybe they could write down some ideas about how to address this in the mediation.

In the meantime, the second mediator was speaking to the Police Officer about her feelings. They discussed the way the session was going and concluded that perhaps Andrea was misunderstanding her questions as interrogatory rather than a way for the Police Officer to understand her actions.

The outcome

At everyone's agreement, the session was resumed. The Police Officer began by apologising to Andrea for making her feel uncomfortable. She then explained the reasons behind her questions and told Andrea of her protective feelings on the night of the incident. She also explained that she had daughters around Andrea's age and only did what she would have wanted someone to do for them in that situation. Andrea then told the Police Officer that she was genuinely sorry about the assault. She explained that she was that she was under the influence of alcohol and feared that her drink had been interfered with. She said that she understood how upsetting it must have been for the Police Officer's children to learn that their mum had been assaulted.

After the session, both participants said they felt better and they could now draw a line under the incident.

Section 5

Serving a custodial sentence

CASE 33 Arson – seeing the emotional consequences of a burnt-out home

14 year old boy set fire to some paper which was thrown by another boy and started a major house fire.

The Youth Offending Team officer referred the case to the partnership agency at the pre-sentence report stage of proceedings. Will was 14 years old and had been involved with 3 others clowning around outside some houses. One boy said to one of the others 'have you got a light?' Will lit the piece of paper that was subsequently thrown into a house by another person who was prosecuted (he was older and had a string of previous offences). Will was also prosecuted for arson because he clearly knew when he lit the paper that it was going to be thrown into the house.

I went to see Will and his mum at home. I told Will what mediation was and that we weren't going to make victim contact before sentencing. Will said to me 'you won't make me meet them' and I'd said I wasn't going to make him do anything he didn't want to do.

Will and his mum were quite strung out about what the sentence was going to be and also because there had been an article in the paper about how this woman had lost her home, for which she had no insurance. In real terms all the damage amounted to £80,000.

Will was given a 12 month custodial sentence (in a secure unit, due to his age). When I saw him in the secure unit he was very emotional, and I judged him too fragile to be ready to face the consequences of his crime in a face-to-face mediation. This visit focussed instead on his understanding of his offence because he was hung up about ' I didn't throw this into the house, I just lit it'. When working with young people, if they have trouble in understanding, I try and simplify their understanding. So I talked of the offence in terms of needing

"Will said to me 'you won't make me meet them' and I'd said I wasn't going to make him do anything he didn't want to do."

all the ingredients to make an apple pie. If you had apples and no pastry you just have stewed apples and if you have pastry and no apples you just have a lump of dough. In consequence he could understand "OK, if I hadn't had lit this, there wouldn't have been an offence". Once he could take that on board the next stage towards a mediation was to raise his awareness of how the arson might have affected the victim. By this stage (2nd visit to the secure unit), I'd made an initial visit to the victim, Yvonne.

Yvonne had come back to her house that day just before Christmas with her 3 children to find it burnt out and the floors dripping with the water from the fire brigade's work. Yvonne was pregnant with her 4th child. This was to be her new partner, Howard's first child and he gave the whole family refuge at his house – 30 miles away. When I went to see Yvonne in the town 30 miles away, there was a huge amount of anger, not particularly from her but from her partner, Howard, who wanted to know what Will was going to do to repay £80,000 of damage.

There had been a huge impact on all the family. The 2 school aged children had to move schools. In the school that they'd had to go to, they had to have showers after games. For one of the girls this proved to be enormously traumatic because her association with the shower was seeing all the water dripping through the ceiling in the house having been burnt down, with the fire brigade having to put it out.

"Can you tell me if you think that a young boy of 14 can understand those large amounts of money?"

Instead of focussing on Yvonne's feelings in relation to the cost I encouraged her to focus on her personal experience and her children's experiences of it. (Will's understanding of money could be simplified as how far a fiver will go). Yvonne had said "I am angry, I am hurt, I'm upset because its costing me large amounts of money" and I had replied "Can you tell me if you think that a young boy of 14 can understand those large amounts of money?"

She said she couldn't. What he could understand was things such as the fact that all the photographs of the children as babies had been burnt – so there were no visual memories, no pictures, no videos of them. In relaying this information (with permission) to Will it proved to be very powerful because Will knew that his mum had a video of him as a baby and photographs of him on the wall. He was greatly saddened that Yvonne would never be able to show people photographs of her children as babies. She was pregnant with the new baby and there would be photographs of that new baby but never of her other children as babies.

When Will expressed his understanding of Yvonne's feelings at this point, I asked him how he could tell this woman that he was listening to what she was saying. He decided he would write and we went through bullet points of things we would include in the letter. I then relinquished the responsibility for doing that to him. His key worker at the secure unit agreed to help him with it as it wasn't something that could be done in just half an hour, but over a period of time. I briefed her about everything She supported him with the writing of the letter. As with all people I always check if there are any literacy issues but there weren't in this case. I received the letter and checked it over to check it wasn't likely to make the victim feel guilty or contain other possible 're-victimising' material.

When I had delivered the letter to Yvonne, she read it whilst I was there and said that she wanted to write back to Will. So I agreed that I would take a letter back to him. She decided to write "you are a really good boy for listening to how things have affected my family and I appreciate that you'd had some pain through all this."

"You are a really good boy for listening to how things have affected my family and I appreciate that you'd had some pain through all this"

She wrote that if she'd been his mother she'd be upset if her son was in a secure unit at Christmas and not with the family. Yvonne also wrote "please don't allow this crime to be the thing that drags you down in life – into a life of offending. Look at your associates, think how upset your mum would be loosing you to the prison service."

I continued to talk to Yvonne and she mentioned that the children had been devastated that the goldfish had been boiled alive and they'd found the goldfish tank melted away. This led to the idea of restoration towards the children. Clearly Will was not going to be able to make any restorative measure in terms of the £80,000 but we looked at what he could do by means of reparation to the children.

After 3 months in the secure unit, Will had his first opportunity to go out of the unit for a few hours and visit his home and his mum. Instead, he went with his key worker to buy 2 new goldfish and gravel and a fish bowl with his pocket money. A few days later – having contacted Yvonne to see if she would accept the fish for her children – I went to the secure unit, collected the fish and took them to Yvonne.

Yvonne was becoming more confident that Will's remorse was genuine, that this boy was taking this seriously, and that the exchange of letters and the goldfish had not arisen out of a young offender wishing to score 'brownie' points in the criminal justice system. Yvonne's personal faith was not to add insult to injury but to support where she could. This went against the feelings of her partner Howard who was predominantly very angry that this little "toe rag" could get away with this and nobody could be held to account for it in terms of the finance. Howard didn't think that there was any value in the communication that was taking place between Yvonne and Will.

Yvonne still wanted Will to understand more about the devastation that the family had been through, not just in the financial sense. At the 2nd appointment Yvonne was there on her own. She said she was engaging in mediation for her own needs – not the rest of the family's.

Having given Will Yvonne's first letter, I asked Will what he thought of it. That was when he had decided he'd buy new goldfish. Having delivered the fish I returned to Will with the message that Yvonne felt that if he was a young man who could have give up that visit to his mum in order to go and buy goldfish, then she was absolutely delighted with that and wished him well. As I was rounding things up with him he asked "do you think I could see the lady?" You could have knocked me down with a feather!

So once back at my office, I phoned Yvonne and said "how would you feel about coming across to meet with Will?". I explained that the meeting would have to be at the secure unit and she said "Yes". A couple of days before the meeting Will rang his mum and told her he was going to meet the woman whose house he'd burnt down. His mum

"As I was rounding things up with him he asked ' do you think I could see the lady?' You could have knocked me down with a feather!."

panicked and rang the Principal of the unit to try to stop the meeting. I was contacted by the unit and telephoned Will's Mum (I'd met her once before pre sentence). I gave her a resume of the whole thing and told her how proud she could be of Will for engaging in this way – it is not every 14 year old that can face the consequences of his actions. I felt it was going the right way. She asked whether she could be there and I said, "Yes, but could we discuss whether that would be the best thing to do?" I explained that Will had done all this of his own volition and asked how she would feel about leaving him to have this meeting to prove himself – he could be a much stronger person because of it. I explained that his key worker would be there and asked if she would like to consider it and get back to me in the afternoon. Will's mum then said "No, I don't need to think about it. I trust you and I jumped in because that was my mother's instinct." So, when she realised that it wasn't going to be confrontational and that it had been at his behest in the first place, she could see the sense in Will continuing on his own.

I'd offered to give Yvonne a lift to the face-to-face meeting but she decided to come on her own. For the face-to-face meeting I was joined by a co-mediator, who had been supervising my mediation work on this case to date. The face-to-face meeting was hugely emotional. For Will and Yvonne, seeing each other was so powerful that they both dissolved into tears, before very few words had been said. Throughout the face-to-face there was very little alluded to in terms of the mediation to date or to the offence. What the face-to-face actually did for Will was allow him to cry, and allow him to release a lot of pent-up emotion. For Yvonne the meeting allowed her to humanise the offender and to say to herself "This has happened to me. Shit does happen, but I can't let it get me down for the rest of my life. I've got to move forward and I've got to feel that I've contributed in some way in helping him not go down that life of crime."

"I've got to move forward and I've got to feel that I've contributed in some way in helping him not go down that life of crime."

Yvonne told Will how brave he'd been, how strong he was and how she felt for his mum. She said she really believed in his resolve not to commit crimes again, because he had now seen how the impact of such a small action had been enormous. The ramifications of it had been just endless and in reality Yvonne wasn't going to recover in a financial sense for a long time. But she said was recovering from her hate and her disappointment in young people in general, and she felt that her involvement was going to help put him back on the right tracks. So Yvonne offered him all her best wishes and luck for the future, and gave her assurance that she believed he had good in him and he wasn't going to commit further offences.

Will cried a lot. I offered him time out, but he said no, he wanted to stay. I asked him why he was crying and he just said it was because he was so sorry. He wasn't mature enough to say "because I'm facing this woman whose house I've burnt down" but "sorry" said it all.

When the tears subsided, Yvonne asked questions that showed her interest in his life, asking what he liked and what he looked forward to when he left custody. He talked about his rugby team, and how he might have lost his place in that team. He was able to talk a bit and answer questions and back off from the absolute emotion. He talked about his release and going back to school, knowing that it would be hard because people would know where he'd been. His mum had said they would have a late Christmas dinner when he came out. I drew the mediation to a close because everyone had said what they had to say, we'd had the emotion and we knew we'd be labouring the point otherwise. There was no need for an agreement because they were not making promises to each other. I offered them the opportunity to shake hands, I believe hugely in human touch, and they did shake hands.

I suggested that Will might like to spend a few minutes with his key worker and I'd see him in a few minutes when I'd debriefed Yvonne. As Will came round and passed her on her side of the table she said "Can I give you a hug?". They hugged and Will left the room with his key worker.

I asked Yvonne if she was OK about going home, and it turned out her partner, Howard, had brought her across and he was going to take her home. I asked Yvonne if she wanted me to speak to Howard and explain the emotion she'd just gone through, she said no, it was fine she'd speak to him herself. My co-mediator asked Yvonne if there was any thing she wanted clarity on or anything she didn't want included in our closing report, but she was fine with it. I suggested that I would give her a quick ring in a month's time to see if she was OK.

Then we went to see Will. We were full of praise of him, and I promised that I'd tell his mum how the meeting went. We thought he was an enormously brave young man and that he'd got a lot of guts. It took an extra special person to meet and face that kind of thing. We asked him if he felt that it would have gone that way. He said no, he hadn't expected to cry, and we suggested to him that his grief was not just about meeting Yvonne, but was also about of where he was. (We were giving him validation for his crying). We asked him if there was anything he hadn't said and he said, no he was OK. We said by all means talk to his mum about it next time he had the opportunity. I said I'd give him a quick call in a month, just before his release, to see he was OK.

I went to see Wills mum and told her all about it. I told her how brave he'd been and how proud she could be of him. She cried. 2 days later I received a card from his mum saying that she was sure that the meeting had made a big difference to Will. Inside was a letter she hoped I might pass to Yvonne. This said "thank you for seeing my son, I'm sure that having met him you'll realise he's not the bad lad you thought he might have been in the first place". The letter also said "As his mum I can say that whatever he said to you he believes. He does have a loving family to come home to and that we thank you for expressing your thoughts to him as it can't have been easy for you".

"As his mum I can say that whatever he said to you he believes. He does have a loving family to come home to and that we thank you for expressing your thoughts to him as it can't have been easy for you."

The letter also said that she was desperately sorry for Yvonne's loss and gave her assurances to support Will in his resolve to change his behaviour. The letter wished Yvonne and her family well.

My task was now to phone Yvonne, tell her that I had the letter, and ask if she would like to receive it. I gave her an overview of the letter before she agreed to it. I was concerned in case the letter could be read as a request or a demand for Yvonne to forgive Will. I didn't want to drag things on and there was no need for Yvonne to accept a letter which I explained could otherwise just stay on file. I didn't want her to feel she had to have another visit from me if it wasn't necessary. The tone of the letter was that mum was being a mum, saying Will wasn't a bad lad etc. She was praising the victim for being prepared to see that side of him. As it happened, following my precis of the letter, Yvonne was very happy for me just to send it to her. I then said, "If you've got any questions just give me a call about it."

I wrote a letter to Will's mum saying I'd sent the letter after checking that the Yvonne wanted to receive it. I thanked Will's mum for her comments and her card and said that I wished them well for when Will was released.

It was a privilege to be part of this process which had involved indirect mediation, reparation and then direct mediation. It had started off with such anger and hurt from the victim and with a resistance to accepting responsibility on the part of the offender. It had progressed onto the offender taking on a lot of responsibility for the emotional impact of his crime and also for his own future.

Reflections

- The success was to focus on the emotional content and the tangible issues that a young boy could relate to.
- Without mediation the victim-awareness work that would have been undertaken with this young offender would be unlikely to have had the same effect on his likelihood of re-offending.
- The mediation work saved other criminal justice staff (Youth Offending Team workers and Probation) much time.
- The need to keep the parents of a young offender informed is paramount. Their attendance at face-to-face restorative meetings is not.
- This service operates the principle that mediation is not held at a time when it might be seen to be being engaged in by offenders because they might get a lesser sentence or early release from custody. Contact can usefully occur pre-sentence but not mediating until after sentencing worked well in this case.

CASE 34 Manslaughter – who is communicating with who?

A 17 year old was convicted of the manslaughter of his friend. Three generations of 'secondary' victims were apparent.

The victim, Gary, was a 17 year old who died as a result of an offence of manslaughter, and the offender, Jimmy, was a 17 year old male. The case came to us when we were giving information to the family about sentence. It was Gary's auntie who came forward to represent the family. The offence had devastated the family and Gary had died in what appeared to be a very brief fight that had happened between the two lads at Gary's grandma's home very late at night.

Grandma, Iris, (who worked nights) came home just as the ambulance was leaving with the body. From then on grandma cut herself off completely and wouldn't draw the curtains that look out onto the front of the house, where Gary died.

It was a few weeks after sentence when the Auntie, Eileen, came forward and said that she had to represent the family because Gary's sister, Sharon, and Gary's Mum, Bev, were absolutely devastated. As well as having been the victim's sister, Sharon was also the girlfriend of the offender, Jimmy.

> *"Iris cut herself off completely and wouldn't draw the curtains that look out onto the front of the house, where her grandson, Gary, died."*

Sharon's aunt Eileen had seen a letter sent from Jimmy (in prison) to Sharon and was very frightened that there was still a relationship between them. Eileen's fear was particularly of the upset that an on-going relationship might cause to Gary's Mum.

Eileen had responded to the victim consultation because she wanted to find out if there was a relationship between Jimmy and Sharon, and if there was she wanted it stopped. We had to say "there's nothing we can do about that, we can't stop a relationship, that's not what we're about."

I then said "However, what we can do is follow up the letter you have written to Jimmy in prison telling him about the impact that the manslaughter had had on the family".

We could see whether he would want to reply to the letter. So we said we would go to prison and see him and see if anything may be done to help repair some of the feelings that were going around in the family.

"As well as having been the victim's sister, Sharon was also the girlfriend of the offender, Jimmy."

We had to say "there's nothing we can do about that, we can't stop a relationship, that's not what we're about."

Jimmy's sentence was three and a half years, so he was probably going to be released within 20 months. In visiting Jimmy, we mediators found him difficult to talk to, monosyllabic and frightened of opening up.

However, when it was made clear by us that Eileen had told us about the letter she had sent, he went straight to his cell and brought it. It was clear that he had opened it on many, many occasions. The letter came out of the envelope at a certain page which was a very poignant description of the last time the family had seen Gary alive and then of their visit to the mortuary.

Jimmy was very anxious about answering the letter because he was concerned about what Eileen or Bev knew of her daughter's involvement in the lead up to the offence and that he might cause even more damage within the family than he'd already done. Jimmy wanted it known that the offence was a tragic accident arising out of a doorstep confrontation and the pulling of a knife. Where the knife came from had not been clearly established in court and what had been said in court was contested by Jimmy. Slowly

"In visiting Jimmy, we found him difficult to talk to, monosyllabic and frightened of opening up."

it became clearer that Jimmy didn't want the family to hear him as saying 'this wasn't my fault'. He wasn't saying that; he was saying that there were reasons why it happened and he couldn't explain these – or rather he could, but was terrified of doing so.

Jimmy's family hadn't dared attend the court because – though no one gave any details of any intimidation having occurred – they felt intimidated by Gary's family. Jimmy had felt unsupported through the long court proceedings. He was frequently upset by the testimony of other people in court when he heard their words as lies.

Jimmy wanted it known that Sharon had instigated the on-going communication between the two of them, not him. Sharon had written "You did kill my brother, but I know you weren't responsible for some of those things said in court and it must all be awful."

After visiting Jimmy my colleague thought there was little ground for hope that there were messages that could safely be exchanged. However he had taken up the offer of a second visit and when we returned Jimmy had already started to write a reply but had got really stuck on some questions that he thought Sharon needed to answer. We indicated that we would be in contact with Eileen again soon and asked if there were any messages he would like us to convey? He asked if he could let her know that he was really sorry for what had happened and that he was sad to have lost one of his friends.

"You did kill my brother, but I know you weren't responsible for some of those things said in court and it must all be awful."

When we visited Eileen she started by telling us that our coming to talk to her before had been really useful for her. She was relieved to have had the opportunity to talk to us and valued the fact that we had been prepared to go and talk to Jimmy. Eileen had started to see that there were things that were going on between these youngsters and rules between youngsters about who said who said what and to whom. As mediators we were glad that Eileen had identified that there were dialogues other than with Jimmy that could move on the understanding of the circumstances of the offence and the impact on a number of people. Eileen asked if we could talk to certain of the young people and said that she thought it would be helpful for them to talk to us too. She made way for us to talk to her own daughter and her sister's daughter at her house.

To summarise the outcomes of the next stage of the mediation work, it was apparent that communication between all the young people and the adults was unlikely to progress far because of the offending-related issues that would need to be said for the whole truth to come out. When I think as to whether it mattered to me whether that communication occurred, I conclude that it didn't matter to me, because as a mediator, I don't own the problems, they do.

Nor does it give me a sense of a job not being completed because I'm there to facilitate their communication, not there to know everything and not their to prise it all out of them for my satisfaction. I only need sufficient information to be able to enable them to operate well.

I do think that these kids coped very well with what they were doing, and I didn't need to know all the ins and outs. Our dialogue with the young people led to a letter being handed over. We always read any letter that we will pass over - this one was written in code.

All we need to do is assure ourselves that there is a minimal risk

> *"When I think as to whether it mattered to me whether that communication occurred, I conclude that it didn't matter to me, because as a mediator, I don't own the problems, they do."*

of emotional or physical harm arising out of delivery of the letter. We were able to satisfy ourselves that this was the case despite all the words that aren't in dictionaries, short-hand and aliases/tags used in the letter. Then a second letter was handed to us in which, more intelligibly, Sharon wrote that she hadn't foreseen that things might end in someone dying. She never dreamed what would actually happen. Sharon was making a semi-apology for her behaviour in relation to that night. There was

> *We always read any letter that we will pass over – this one was written in code.*

also some acknowledgement that she knew what she was doing. When we handed Jimmy the letter during a visit to the prison it was apparent that there was information in it that was new to him, and hard for him to absorb. However with a bit of time to think he then felt able to write back to Gary's Aunt Eileen.

Now that Sharon had admitted to him that there was a 'set-up' that night and expressed some kind of remorse, he could forgive the set up and it helped him to take responsibility.

My co-mediator was astonished, as she hadn't thought Jimmy was going to be capable of doing that. His whole communication style had changed startlingly from the monosyllabic withdrawn 17 year old we had met in prison a few months earlier.

When we took the letter Jimmy had written to Eileen back to her we found ourselves needing to dampen the surprise we experienced on finding that she didn't want the letter replying to her questions. Eileen didn't need the letter at that point. She had needed to write a letter earlier but now she wanted to be out of communication and putting her attention elsewhere; she had moved on. Eileen was glad that some communication was happening between the youngsters and she felt the issue lay more with them anyway. This process – from the initial letter from Auntie to try and stop the relationship – had taken 8 to 9 months by the time we'd taken letters back and forth and they'd thought about them and what they wanted to say. The time the participants needed to reflect between communications was what determined the pace of the communication; and there inevitably was a slight delay in terms of the logistics of our shuttling the letters.

"His whole communication style had changed startlingly from the monosyllabic withdrawn 17 year old we had met in prison a few months earlier."

Eileen had had to accept that no-one can stop a relationship other than those within it and she'd had to start thinking about why she was worried about it. The youngsters have all had to think about it and how they're going to live together afterwards. Now that Eileen had accepted that this has more to do with the kids than with anybody else, the mediators task was to relay that information appropriately.

Jimmy said that even though Eileen didn't want the letter he was glad he had written it to say what he wanted to say about the court and the lies. He found himself involved in a lot of communication with his contemporaries who were all over 17 years old. This communication was not known to the parents and carers.

When Jimmy came up for release there was a complicated set of communications that were facilitated sometimes with and sometimes without the mediators.

(Space being short, the rest of the story awaits publication in a book following-on from this one. *Ed*)

Reflections

• If the 'secret communication' known to the mediators had involved someone under 17 the mediators would have had to consider more closely any obligation to let others know what communication was taking place and any need for the consent of parents/carers.

• Where the offender is a friend or relative of the victim, there will often be many others who have to come to terms with how the crime impacts on their relationship to the offender. Though a multi-party meeting was not part of this case, at an appropriate stage a multi-party victim-offender mediation would have been offered. It would not have been a beginning process or an end process, but interspersed with checking out on one-to-one basis the extent to which the participants were clear about their needs and how they felt about the choices which might meet those needs.

CASE 35 **Street robbery in a small community**

A 17 year old male robbed a former female schoolmate. Both victim and offender lived in the same small village and contact between them was inevitable.

Annette, a 17 year old A level student, was assaulted and robbed in the street by Brian, a 17 year old former schoolmate. She was left traumatised by the offence and sought counselling. Brian was sentenced to 18 months in custody and released on licence, electronically tagged, a year after the offence.

The Restorative Justice Service received the referral from the Probation Service Victim Contact Officer (who visits all victims whose offenders are sentenced to one year or more in custody). Both Annette and Brian lived in the same small village and, after Brian's release, had seen each other in the area and had dealt with this by avoidance – walking away, changing routes, no eye contact and so on.

By this time Annette had gone on to university but returned home regularly. Brian lived with his family half a mile away. Annette's mother worked in the only local shop and contact between the families was inevitable.

Restorative Justice workers contacted both parties. Issues identified were:

- Annette wondered if she had been targeted because, at school, she had been seen as passive and easily manipulated.
- Annette blamed herself to a degree. She should not have been openly fiddling with her handbag. Would Brian blame her for his sentence?
- Brian accepted responsibility for the offence and did not hide behind his drug use. He wanted to apologise but was afraid he would be seen as insincere.
- Families were initially suspicious of each other but eventually became supportive. However, friends tried to dissuade both from having anything to do with each other, or the mediation process.
- Each party stated they wanted what the other party wanted. 'I will if he/she wants to' meant that neither was keen to say what they wanted to happen.

Over several months, restorative justice practitioners worked with both parties, encouraging expression of what each wanted, passing on feelings, fears etc. Emotion-laden letters were exchanged which both parties welcomed and responded to with frankness. The process was slow, inevitably delayed by Annette's absence at university and Brian's return to prison to have his electronic tag removed.

Eventually, after four months, both parties agreed to a direct meeting. This took place in a local church hall, overseen by experienced restorative justice practitioners

The formal structure for such meetings was soon seen to be inappropriate as both Annette and Brian reacted very naturally to each other, after some initial embarrassed shyness. Annette spoke with feeling of her anger, hurt and loss of self esteem, while Brian explained his actions without excusing or justifying them in any way. He explained, as he had previously done by letter, that he had not targeted Annette because of his past knowledge of her. Such was his need

Over several months, restorative justice practitioners worked with both parties, encouraging expression of what each wanted

for money to buy drugs that the victim could have been anybody. He was very moved by Annette's account of her response to the offence. His remorse was seen as genuine and his sincere apology accepted by Annette. They both expressed satisfaction with the process and signed the following agreement:

1. Brian genuinely apologises to Annette for all the upset he caused her.
2. Annette accepts Brian's apology and forgives him.
3. In future they will behave naturally towards each other. They will speak if meeting by chance. They hope to rebuild their past friendship.

Separately Annette and Brian thanked the restorative justice workers and some days later a card was received from Annette, profuse in her thanks.

Judging by perceived participant satisfaction in making and receiving apology we believe this case (like the vast majority) to be a success.

Reflections

- Factors leading to success were:
    a. Both parties were committed to the process and accepted that, given they were bound to continue to meet, something had to be sorted out.
    b. Supportive families.
    c. Staff had time and resources to persist despite some setbacks.
    d. Good links with the supervising Probation Officer and Victim Contact Officer.
- One problem in progressing with the case arose from the offender having a licence condition forbidding contact with the victim. This was resolved with the supervising Probation Officer. In an ideal restorative justice world, mediation could have helped at point of sentence and possibly saved the victim many months of trauma.
- Post release from custody can often be a very constructive time for victim-offender mediation to take place.

CASE 36 **Theft from a valued drug support worker**

*A client stole her key worker's purse and
misused her credit card.*

During a home visit, Scarlet, a heroin addict, stole a purse from Mel, her Drug Support Worker. Scarlet had then used her credit card several times. She volunteered for mediation whilst in custody through a self-referral system run in conjunction with the Probation Resettlement Team. She said she wanted to make an apology for what she had done.

Contact with the parties

Scarlet was visited in prison and appeared very sincere in her desire to make an apology. She said she would be willing to have a direct meeting if Mel requested this, but otherwise would like to write a letter of apology. Scarlet said that they had enjoyed a close relationship at the time of the offence and that it preyed on her mind that she had betrayed the trust between them.

Victim contact was requested through the Police Contact Worker. Mel quickly responded and said she was willing to meet with mediators. Mel was delighted to see the mediators when they visited her. She said she had felt close to Scarlet at the time of the offence and had been very upset by what had happened. She also said she did not like to think of Scarlet in prison and of her children in care. She was keen to have a direct meeting, which she felt would enable her to put what had happened behind her and move on.

Scarlet was delighted when she was told how positive Mel had been about the possibility of mediation.

Scarlet said she was strongly in favour of this option and very glad that she would have the opportunity to apologise to Mel and try to make things right between them. It was agreed that mediators would try to organise the meeting before her release date which both Scarlet and Mel felt would be preferable.

Scarlet was delighted when she was told how positive Mel had been about the possibility of mediation.

The mediators had not held a direct meeting in the prison before but the staff were quite helpful in co-operating about the situation. When it was clear that mediators were going to be able to hold the meeting within the prison, they had a second meeting with Mel to go over the format of a direct mediation and explore further her hopes for the meeting. Mel was very clear that this was the right option for her and seemed composed at the idea of meeting with Scarlet again.

The meeting

On the day of the meeting Mel was collected from her home and driven to the prison. The meeting was held in a private room within the Probation Department. A Prison Officer remained in the room with, but was unobtrusive – the mediators ensured she was out of the line of sight of both victim and offender – and she assured us she would not interrupt and would maintain confidentiality.

The meeting started with the usual process of going over ground rules and then each party had a period of 'uninterrupted time' to describe their experience of the offence. This felt somewhat unnecessarily formal as they knew each other before but keeping to the agreed format helped to ensure that the mediation process was effective and did not lose its focus.

The rest of the meeting passed very easily with extended informal communication between both parties that covered the issues they had said they wanted to. Towards the end of the time available mediators brought them back to the focus by suggesting they consider a possible agreement.

Mel had told us previously that she hoped to be able to have further (non-professional) contact with Scarlet and the mediators felt it was important that both parties understood how this might work. The mediators helped devise a written agreement which set out clear boundaries around possible future contact between them. Both parties expressed high satisfaction with having had the mediation process available to clear up personal issues between them that would otherwise have been left unresolved.

Reflections

- The participants expressed satisfaction with the process which indicates that the outcome was successful.

- Both parties were highly motivated to participate in mediation and mediators were able to move quickly to keep the process going at the pace they wanted.

CASE 37 **Burglary with high risk of re-offending**

A prolific offender burgled a young mother's house. The victim and offender met for mediation in prison.

Simon was referred to mediation to explore victim awareness as part of his Supervision Plan. Simon was 26 years old at the time and had received a custodial sentence of 48 months for Burglary. Simon was a prolific offender and had been identified as requiring intense supervision by the Prolific Offender Programme's (POPS) Team at Probation. Simon had been addicted to heroin at the time of his offence, had low self-esteem and he had been assessed by the POP's team as being at high risk of re-offending.

Prior to being given a custodial sentence Simon lived in a run down, closely-knit urban area close to the town centre. Simon lived with his disabled mother and he was her sole carer, a role that had to be taken on by his sister, who lived about 7miles away with her husband and baby.

Mediators sent a letter to Simon to let him know they would be visiting him in prison. When mediators first met Simon he appeared to have taken responsibility for the offence and explained that he had stolen items from a house in his community, a few streets away from his. He explained that he had been a drug user since he was 16 years old and the items he stole were to be sold on to fund his drug habit. He felt embarrassed and ashamed of his behaviour and he wanted to apologise to his victim by letter.

The process of mediation was delayed due to Data Protection. The mediators had to wait for the Police Contact Officer to contact the victim. However, the Police Contact Officer was new to the post and was completing the work for the restorative justice agency in overtime. It was 3 months later that mediators received consent to contact the victim.

The victim's story

The victim, Carina, was very angry about the burglary but she was willing to attend prison to take part in direct mediation with Simon. Mediators visited Carina to explain the process of mediation and to discuss any concerns she had. Carina explained that she had been in the process of moving into the house after she had separated from her husband. Although the house was not fully furnished she had been storing items there and she had been visiting the house everyday to decorate. At the time of the offence she had just popped out to get some wallpaper. The burglary had caused Carina much distress and made her feel vulnerable, particularly as she was going to be living alone with her young child. Carina had a number of questions she wanted answers to and she wanted to know what had happened to a certain piece of jewellery that had been very precious to her.

Another visit was arranged to see Simon. As he was willing to take part in indirect mediation, the mediators wanted to see how he felt about taking part in face-to-face mediation in prison. Simon appeared very keen to participate and mediators explained that Carina was very angry with him and *She wanted to know what had happened to a certain piece of jewellery that had been very precious to her.* wanted to tell him this. Mediators gave Simon a typed sheet of questions that Carina wanted answers to, and explained that he could answer these questions during the meeting.

Both parties agreed to the direct mediation taking place in the prison environment and mediators liaised with probation staff at the prison to organise a suitable room. The mediators collected Carina from her home and on the way to the prison, they discussed the format of the meeting. Carina was still very angry and fired up ready to tell Simon how she had been affected by the offence.

The meeting

When they arrived at the prison, the mediators and Carina had to undergo the normal prison procedure for entry, which involved numerous security checks. The mediators were aware of Carina becoming anxious as they waited at each check-point. The mediators discovered the problem with holding a direct mediation in prison was the lack of control over the environment. They were eventually shown to a room where the professional visits take place and this gave them the privacy they required.

One of the mediators waited outside the room for Simon to arrive and the other mediator helped to settle Carina and organise the room. When Simon arrived the mediator thanked both parties for taking part, acknowledging how brave they both were. During the meeting Simon became very upset and he was given time out. After a short pause, he carried on and Carina told mediators afterwards that she had to fight back her tears, especially when Simon broke down.

During the meeting Simon gave Carina a letter of apology, which she read stating that it was self-explanatory. She also asked if she could write a letter back to Simon in response, the mediators agreed to pass on the letter on. The meeting ended and both victim and offender appeared to have benefited from taking part in the process.

One of the mediators collected the letter from Carina and posted it to Simon with a note asking him how he felt post-mediation. Simon wrote back thanking the mediators for all their help and support during the past 5 months. He stated that he felt he had undergone a transformation. Mediators spoke with Carina post-mediation and she felt as though she had benefited from the experience in that she had a better understanding of Simon's offending behaviour and her questions had been answered.

Reflections

- The direct mediation was very successful. This can be judged by the feedback given by both victim and offender.
- Issues that assisted in the success of the case were; the offender had taken responsibility for his offence, both parties were willing and probation staff at the prison were very helpful.
- If the offender had gone through a 'transformation' by taking part in a direct meeting with his victim, it may prevent him from re-offending, enabling him to face up to the effects of his behaviour. This will save the Criminal Justice System money and time in the future.
- The way the Data Protection Act is interpreted in our locality allows only a Police Officer to make contact with victims of crime and this meant that the mediators had to wait 3 months for victim contact in this case. In the past when mediators have received victim consent, if it has

taken a few months, the offender has often changed their mind about participating in the process, which is then frustrating for the victim.

CASE 38 Indecent assault on a young girl

A 15 year old boy indecently assaulted a young girl and physically assaulted her friend. The victim requested a meeting with the offender.

Lee was a 15-year-old boy with no previous criminal history. He lived with his mother and a younger brother. He saw his father occasionally, and although it was not obvious, he had been more upset by the recent break up of his parent's marriage than most people realised. Lee was a student at a local school, but his attendance and achievements were poor. His self-esteem was low.

Katie was a vibrant 12-year-old girl. Being brought up by a doting mum and protecting brothers, (her father worked abroad for many months of the year) she showed maturity beyond her years and exuded confidence.

The offence

One afternoon, Katie had been playing on some wasteland near to her home with her two friends, Claire and Daniel, both of whom were in Katie's class at school. They had been walking Daniel's dog.

The three were talking, laughing and playing. They became aware that someone was standing close by, watching them. It was Lee. He was holding a golf club, and, unbeknown to the three children, he was convinced that they were laughing at him.

Lee approached Katie, Claire and Daniel and angrily demanded to know what they were laughing at. Katie told him that they were just playing. Lee's manner was menacing and the 3 were frightened.

Lee told Claire and Daniel to go home but Katie told him that they had to stay together, and offered to help him find his golf ball.

Lee became angry and hit Daniel about the head and body with the golf club. Daniel began to cry, and the dog ran away. Lee told Claire to collect sticks, as many as she could – she was very frightened and began to collect twigs near to Daniel. Lee threatened to kill them all if they spoke about this to anyone.

Lee then led Katie towards a nearby bush, so that they were partially hidden from Claire and Daniel.

Lee asked Katie to kiss him. She refused. Lee wanted to know why she wouldn't kiss him. Katie said "If I kiss you will you let me go?" Lee said that he would.

Katie leaned to give him a brief 'peck' but Lee pulled her towards him and kissed her on the mouth and around her neck. Despite Katie's attempts to break free, Mark held her and continued to kiss her and fondle her over her clothes. He asked her to be his girlfriend.

Katie was terrified. Lee began to open the button and zip on his jeans whilst reiterating the threat to kill them all if she did not comply with his demands. Katie said "You're not going to have sex with me are you?"

Lee exposed himself, and then forced Katie to masturbate him. He also tried to force her to perform oral sex on him. When she showed reluctance he again threatened to kill them all. Katie began to cry. Soon after, Lee ejaculated, and told Katie that he had enjoyed the experience.

Lee then dressed himself and after re-issuing death threats to all three children should they mention any of this to anyone, and laughing at Lucy who had collected a large pile of twigs, then left the scene.

The shocked children cried and supported each other until they got home and told their parents, who in turn contacted the Police.

Lee was subsequently arrested, positively identified, and after the trial, was sentenced to a 3 year Detention and Training Order.

A request to meet

A year later, the Prison Victim Contact Team wrote to a Restorative Justice Worker with the Youth Offending Team. The Victim Contact Team had maintained contact with Katie's family and had been told of a request by Katie to meet Lee face-to-face, and to ask him questions about what he did to her and why.

Claire and Daniel had received considerable counselling support following their ordeal, but Katie had refused this, believing that a face-to-face meeting with Lee was the only way to restore her self esteem and confidence.

The Restorative Justice Worker (a Police Constable) agreed to make contact with Katie and her family to explore any options available.

Katie, now 13 years came across as courageous and determined. The only signs of vulnerability came when the details of the offence were broached.

Restorative principles were discussed and it became clear that Katie possessed the strengths and capabilities needed to participate in such a meeting. Her mother, Pat, although naturally apprehensive, was fully supportive of her daughter, and was also a willing participant.

The Police Constable made it very clear to Katie and Pat right from the beginning that such a meeting could only take place if Lee, who had recently been released on Licence, was also a willing participant.

The Police Constable liaised with prison staff to ensure that adequate support was available to Lee before, during and after the meeting.

The Police Constable then made arrangements to visit Lee who was living at home with his mother. Lee was now 17 years old and was alone at home when two workers made the initial visit. Once the reason for the visit had been explained to Lee he was asked to consider whether he would like to take part in such a meeting "If it will help her, I'll do it" he said.

Lee did not want his mother or any family member to be present at the meeting and was happy for a Restorative Justice Worker to be his supporter.

However, 3 weeks later, Lee was arrested for a serious, unrelated offence and was subsequently sentenced to a further 3 year custodial sentence.

Katie was kept informed and following the sentence said "Oh OK. So that means the meeting will be in prison? Good."

The Police Constable explained that Lee's attitude towards the meeting may have changed, and that once he had 'settled back' into prison life she would approach him again.

Several weeks after the latter sentence began, the Restorative Justice Workers visited Lee in prison. When the subject of the meeting was mentioned, Lee, once again said "If it will help her, I'll do it."

Several months of preparation between Lee and Katie then followed.

For Katie it clearly evoked emotions that had been previously suppressed, in particular her fears about her mother's ability to cope with the meeting. Pat clearly benefited from the extra support, and the process strengthened the already strong bond between mother and daughter.

The Police Constable liaised with prison staff to ensure that adequate support was available to Lee before, during and after the meeting.

Katie had a number of questions that she wanted to ask of Lee, and the Police Constable helped her to turn angry statements into constructive questions, typing them in bold print.

The meeting

Katie visited the prison prior to the meeting, with her Mother, and the 2 Restorative Justice Workers.

Katie chose which room she wanted the meeting to take place, where she wanted to sit and which door Lee was to enter from.

Almost 2 years on the day of the meeting arrived. Katie seemed calm and focused. Pat was very nervous.

Meticulous planning ensured that arrangements at the prison went like clockwork.

Lee, although extremely nervous, answered all 16 of Katie's questions with astonishing honesty and sincerity.

The power balance was an extremely important issue to Katie, and Lee conceded that Katie was the ultimate victor as she had her freedom and the support of her family – he had neither.

The genuineness of Lee's apology was heart-rending to all present. He told us that he was disgusted with himself and would never do anything like that again.

Pat, whose anger towards Lee since the indecent assault offence was never far from the surface, felt the need to privately ask Katie's permission to describe to Lee how Katie would sit in boiling hot water, in the bath, scrubbing herself clean until she bled following the offence.

Pat later said that she had found it difficult to maintain her anger once she realised that Lee was giving her daughter the empowerment she had longed for.

Pat later said that she had found it difficult to maintain her anger once she realised that Lee was giving her daughter the empowerment she had longed for. A contract relating to confidentiality and post release contact was signed by all present at Katie's request.

Both Katie and Pat thanked Lee for agreeing to meet them. Pat also wished him well for his future, and hoped that in time his family would accept him back again.

Lee was thoroughly de-briefed by the Restorative Justice Workers and prison staff, during which he asked the Police Constable if he could talk to a Police colleague about several outstanding matters.

"I had not realised that Katie's sparkle had gone, it is now back with a vengeance, together with her self esteem and confidence!"

Katie's jubilation was tangible, particularly during the journey home. She was overjoyed that Lee had answered all of her questions so fully, and that he had acknowledged her bravery in requesting and attending this meeting.

3 weeks after the meeting the Police Constable received a "Thank You" card from Pat. She wrote "I had not realised that Katie's sparkle had gone, it is now back with a vengeance, together with her self esteem and confidence!"

Lee is due for release on licence in 6 months time.

Reflections

• This was a successful case as both parties experienced some closure on a serious and distressing incident. The victim felt empowered by the experience. The victim's mother's anger ebbed away, and the offender felt that he had helped to restore some of the harm caused by his offending. This is judged by the feedback from all parties during de-briefing.

• Issues that assisted the success of the case were the meticulous planning of the venue, timing, and liaison with prison personnel. Another contributory factor was the thorough preparation of all parties concerned. The Restorative Justice Worker also gained valuable support from contact with other more experienced practitioners in other areas.

• The restorative approach prevented the need for counselling support for

Katie and Pat which may have been inevitable for both without this approach. It is also believed (and hoped) that Lee's offending will reduce (or cease) following this process.

- Existing laws or guidelines did not make it difficult to work in a restorative way. However, a national campaign to raise awareness of RJ would assist a great deal in the planning and preparation of such events.

Section 6

Post custody (on licence)

CASE 39 Rape: communication between brother and sister

An 18 year old raped his 13 year old sister.
The victim and her mother sought
communication with the offender.

Shaun – aged 18 at the time of the offence – was convicted a year later of raping his sister, Daniella, who was aged 13 at the time of the offence. Shaun, after being held on remand, was sentenced to two years in custody and an extended licence period of two years on probation supervision. When released from custody Shaun was discharged to a probation hostel.

The Probation Officer referred the case to mediators. Two mediators worked on this case throughout. Shaun's mother, Sandra, had been in contact with the probation service because she has not had any contact with her son since the offence. Shaun's mother said that Daniella wanted to meet with Shaun. Sandra said that Daniella wanted to meet him to tell him how sad she'd felt and how she needed to move on.

The first contact between the mediators and Daniella took place after communication with her Social Worker, who checked that Daniella was willing to see the mediators. When Daniella was visited at home she said she wanted to establish contact with her brother to ask him why he raped her. She also wanted him to know that he is still her brother and she loves him, but doesn't like what he did to her.

She also wanted to hear him admit to having raped her. She said she needed this to help her move on.

The mediators later agreed that they had picked up a feeling that she felt guilty about reporting him, because he had then served a prison sentence. It had been important to stress to Daniella during the first visit that mediation was a voluntary process and that she needed to prepare herself for the fact that Shaun might not want anything to do with her, that he might still be in denial of the offence and Daniella might not get to hear what she expected to hear and wanted to hear. She accepted that.

The mediators went to visit Shaun in the probation hostel with his *"she wanted to establish contact with her brother to ask him why he raped her. She also wanted him to know that he is still her brother and she loves him, but doesn't like what he did to her"*

Support Worker from the hostel present. The Support Worker had told us before the visit that Shaun was very distressed by the offence and the sentence and was also very anxious about seeing his sister in town. Shaun had questions of his own that he wanted to ask. Shaun did not deny that he had had sex with his 13 year old sister but maintained that it was consensual. Despite having pleaded guilty in court, he could not accept that he was guilty of rape because he felt she instigated the situation and gave out the wrong signals.

During the visit the mediation process was explained to him, that it is voluntary and that the referral had come from Daniella via her Social Worker and that had gone through the Probation Officer. Shaun was told that the mediators were not in judgement of either party. At that point he relaxed a little. Later on in the discussion Shaun expressed his view that rape is a violent act on a stranger, for example in a park and that he didn't think he had been violent or unpleasant to Daniella. He didn't consider himself a rapist. The dialogue then involved explaining to Shaun that rape is not necessarily violent but that it is non-consensual. In discussing the concept of consent, Shaun was left to think about whether in her own mind Daniella had consented.

Shaun then said that in his mind what he'd done that was wrong was just that he'd had sex with his sister. He also claimed that Daniella was having another intra-family sexual relationship. The mediators clarified that whether Daniella had had sex with another family member was not relevant to Shaun being charged with rape, because she hadn't reported it. He had been charged with rape because Daniella had reported that he had had non-consensual sex with her.

The mediators then relayed messages from Daniella that she still loved him and that she valued him as a brother. There was also the message from Shaun's mother that she still loved him and that she'd agreed that she wouldn't try and hit him if he agreed to a meeting with his sister. At that point Shaun began to cry and said that he missed his family. At this point the mediators chose to take a break. After the break, Shaun said he needed time to think about all the issues because he was confused and needed time to sort out his own feelings. The visit ended by establishing the arrangements for a further visit from the mediators.

At the second visit to Shaun, he expressed that he wanted his family to know that he changed his plea from not guilty to guilty because he didn't want the family put through more pain and torn apart by court appearances. If Shaun had pleaded not guilty, his sister would have had to have gone to court. He had said to his Solicitor that he was saving his sister from having to give evidence and that by admitting guilt he was able to protect the family.

Shaun went on to say that he wanted to ask of his mother why she had not visited him whilst in prison. He said that all the time he was in there nobody visited him. The dialogue between the mediators and Shaun relayed the family feelings towards him now and Shaun became more upset. Shaun wanted to express what he had lost and express all his feelings about what had happened since he was charged. After talking about his experience of being in custody, Shaun asked if he would be able to phone his mother. Shaun wanted to know how his family was and asked if had the mediators had seen his younger brother.

Shaun said that he didn't think he would be able to cope with any meeting with his sister because he was ashamed and he wanted the family to know that he loved them all and missed them. The mediators agreed with Shaun that they would go and see his mother separately because they had got separate issues and would get back to Shaun once they had seen his mother and sister again.

Mediation with Shaun's mother

The mediators then explained to Shaun's mother how he felt, and she later contacted the mediators to give them a mobile phone into which she'd programmed her own mobile phone number so he could ring her on this, without the rest of the family knowing. The mediators passed this phone to Shaun's Probation Officer, who made sure the phone reached Shaun. This communication channel was made possible by the mediators having told Shaun's mother that he was upset, had cried and that he still loved her, missed her and wanted to know why she hadn't visited him. Shaun's mother wanted to be able to talk to her son and a direct route of communication was established so that they were able to say what they needed to say to one another.

The mediators saw no more role for themselves in relation to Shaun's mother. Though they had tried to encourage everybody to be open and for Shaun's mother to tell Daniella that she had given Shaun a mobile phone. She wouldn't and the mediators had to go along with this because that was her wish. It would have been a lot easier if the family were open about things, but the family had a 'tradition of secrecy' about everything.

The mediators next visit to Daniella relayed to her that he admitted what he had done to her was wrong and his acceptance and that what he had had difficulty accepting was that it was a rape. The mediators were clear that there was a highly problematic lack of congruence in the accounts of what had happened. Total congruence is unrealistic before a face-to-face meeting. However, in this case there were a number of reasons why a face-to-face meeting was inappropriate. The mediators thought that the differences were too great and couldn't be resolved, and Shaun did not want a face-to-face meeting. Also the mediators felt that there were greater gains for all parties possible by continuing the indirect mediation.

The mediators discussed with Daniella how futile a meeting would be if one party was willing and the other one wasn't. Daniella kept saying that she just wanted to ask Shaun a couple of things, so the mediators asked her again what it was she wanted and she went over the point of why Shaun had done it. The mediators said that Shaun had already answered that question.

Daniella wanted Shaun to have some photos of the family and so passed these to the mediators. When these were passed to the probation hostel, the Probation Service policy meant that Shaun was not allowed to be given any photos of his sister as the victim. Daniella was informed that Shaun had gladly received the family photographs that she had sent him, but was disappointed that the staff would not let Shaun have the photos of her. The mediators explained that the staff were responsible for protecting victims and were applying a rule that they would apply for any other rape victim whose photos would not be allowed in a probation hostel.

Shaun had been distressed at the hostel when others had asked him why he had pictures of his mother, dad and brothers by his bed but none of his sister. This information was relayed to Daniella at the final visit. The mediators decided to draw the mediation to a close because no-one was saying anything which implied that progress could be made on the differences in the accounts of the offence. By this stage Shaun had moved out of the probation hostel. The mediators informed Shaun that Daniella still sent the message that she loved him and hoped they could both meet some time. The mediators reminded him that he was still on licence and had a responsibility not to approach her should they meet in the street. Shaun said he was pleased about that because he liked clarity about what he could and couldn't do.

Shaun had moved and he wanted his new telephone number to be passed on to the rest of the family so they could ring him. The family were aware that direct contact between Shaun and his sister was prohibited but still not aware of the the direct telephone link between Shaun and his mother.

Shaun's sentence was completed in 2003 after two years on licence.

Reflections

- Indirect mediation is sometimes more appropriate than face-to-face mediation. The use of indirect mediation enabled more bridges to be built than if it had been a direct mediation in which case the different view of the offence could have broken down the communication that had been built up.
- This case progressed by the mediators being flexible in addressing presenting issues. There had been a number of missed appointments and some unscheduled visits to the mediators' office.
- There was no happy ending to this case but some progress was made in enabling Shaun and his family to have some contact.
- Without direct contact, the victim was able to pass on her love for her brother.
- Shaun had got the assurance that his family still loved him.
- Shaun was able to have a different understanding that non-consensual sex is rape. This is a vital understanding for all young men to learn in their sexual relationships.
- Had the mediators contact with the victim led to the acknowledgement of another offence then further steps would have been taken. If a mediator hears of an offence against a child, they must take action and report it. It is always necessary to report an alleged offence to a mediator's

supervisor and the supervisor can make the decision about reporting it on.

CASE 40 **Robbery of an elderly woman**

A 17 year old boy robbed an elderly woman causing serious injuries. The victim and offender later took part in a film about restorative justice.

Sarah, an elderly woman, was robbed of her handbag in the street during the early evening. She was badly injured in the course of the robbery – although when she spoke about the incident, she always said 'When I fell ……' The offender, Robert, was 17 and a drug addict who needed money for drugs.

Robert began asking questions about how his victim was while he was in prison.

When he was released, with an electronic tag, he asked his Case Manager from the Youth Offending Team if the victim would be prepared to meet him. She was visited by the Restorative Justice Practitioner who had dealt with her initially to obtain a victim perspective for the Pre-Sentence Report. Sarah agreed to meet him.

Robert was visited at home by the Restorative Justice Manager, who discussed the situation with him and his mother (with whom he lived). His mother offered to come with him, but he said that he had to face the meeting by himself. He had been on drugs – the motivation for the robbery was to obtain money for drugs – but had come off them while in prison.

The RJ Manager collected Robert on the day of the meeting. He was very nervous. As they approached the meeting place, they saw the victim with the RJ Practitioner and two others standing

"Robert began asking questions about how his victim was while he was in prison."

outside, so Robert and the RJ Manager waited further up the road until the building was opened.

Sarah had brought with her both her son and her daughter-in-law. The meeting was very calm – Sarah told Robert how the offence had affected her and he told her how he had felt about it while he was in prison, and how he had thought about how he would have felt if it had happened to his own mother. Sarah's son and daughter-in-law both spoke. Her son said he and other relatives had been out on the street on the night of the robbery looking for him and that, if they had found him, they would have attacked him. They would have been prepared to go to jail for this. He had been in prison himself when he was younger and he talked to Robert about that experience.

Sarah's daughter-in-law spoke about the effect on Sarah and about how angry she had been when she visited Sarah in hospital. At the end of the meeting they stood up and Robert and Sarah shook hands. He towered over her but she held on to his hand and asked him never to go back on drugs.

"At the end of the meeting they stood up and Robert and Sarah shook hands. He towered over her but she held on to his hand and asked him never to go back on drugs."

She said that he and his mum were very welcome to come and visit her – they lived close by – and that they could talk about what had happened as she was anxious that his mum should feel able to speak to her.

The Restorative Justice Project was in the course of making a video about its work and asked Sarah and Robert if they would be filmed (anonymously) about the meeting and its impact on them. Sarah agreed, 'if it will help other people who've gone through it', but Robert refused. Some time later, when plans were quite far advanced, the Restorative Justice Manager had a call from Robert's Case Manager to say that he had changed his mind and would be filmed. He and his mum had apparently met Sarah in the street and she had talked about the filming. When he said that he was not going to take part, Sarah asked him to do it for her and he agreed.

Reflections

• The personal contact in mediation can provide the motivation for offenders to think about stopping offending. This then has to be backed up with resources to help offenders change their lives, in this case help with drug addiction.

Selected Reading

- Zehr, H (2002) The Little Book of Restorative Justice, Good Books, Intercourse, Pennsylvania
- Johnstone, G (ed) (2003) A Restorative Justice Reader —Texts, sources, context, Willan Publishing, Cullompton, Devon.
- Wynne, J (2000), "Victim-Offender Mediation in Practice", in Liebmann, M (2000), Mediation in Context, Jessica Kingsley Publishers, London.
- Home Office (2003) Restorative justice: the Government's strategy
  http://www.homeoffice.gov.uk/docs2/restorativestrategy.pdf

Subject Index

Action Plan Order: Case 26, Case 27, Case 28

Actual Apology Letters: Case 12, Case 22

Adult Offenders (Over 18): Case 11, Case 31, Case 37, Case 39

Arson: Case 22, Case 33

Burglary -Commercial Premises: Case 8

Burglary —Domestic: Case 21, Case 37

Caution: Case 3

Community Rehabilitation Order: Case 11, Case 16, Case 31

Community Service Order: Case 30

Criminal Damage: Case 6, Case 10, Case 17, Case 26, Case 29, Case 31

Custody: Case 12, Case 33, Case 34, Case 35, Case 36, Case 37, Case 38, Case 39, Case 40

Drug Issues: Case 1, Case 12, Case 30, Case 31, Case 35, Case 36, Case 37, Case 40

Final Warning: Case 6, Case 7, Case 8, Case 9, Case 10

Learning Difficulties: Case 5, Case 8, Case 15, Case 23

Manslaughter: **Case 34**

Media Coverage: **Case 22**

Public Order Offence: **Case 11, Case 18**

Railways: **Case 25**

Referral Order: **Case 14, Case 15, Case 17, Case 18, Case 19, Case 20, Case 21**

Reparation Order: **Case 25, Case 29, Case 32**

Reprimand: **Case 2, Case 4**

Robbery: **Case 12, Case 13, Case 24, Case 35, Case 40**

School: **Case 1, Case 2, Case 4, Case 6, Case 7, Case 8, Case 13, Case 19, Case 20, Case 22, Case 23, Case 27, Case 31, Case 33, Case 35, Case 36**

Scottish Children's Panel: **Case 5**

Sexual Offences: **Case 15, Case 23, Case 38, Case 39**

Supervision Order: **Case 13, Case 22, Case 23, Case 24**

Taking (Motor Vehicle) Without Owner's Consent: **Case 16**

Theft: **Case 2, Case 3, Case 5, Case 14, Case 36**

Threats: **Case 1**

Violence/Assault: **Case 4, Case 7, Case 9, Case 19, Case 20, Case 27, Case 28, Case 32**

Written Agreement (text): **Case 13, Case 35**

Youth Justice Board News: **Case 26**

Mediation UK – representing and supporting mediation in the community.

Do you have an interesting RJ case?

– and a few minutes to fill this form in? These cases will be used for future publication and/or media work.

Offence Type:

☐ Violence ☐ Robbery ☐ Sexual Offences ☐ Fraud & Forgery

☐ Motoring ☐ Drugs ☐ Other (e.g. Protest Action) _____

☐ Burglary ☐ Theft ☐ Criminal Damage

I am able within one to three months:

1) to submit a full write-up of the case study? (a brief would be supplied) **Yes/No**

2) to be available for interviewing about this case? **Yes/No**

3) to be contacted by Mediation UK's Communication Co-ordinator
   about talking to the media about this case? **Yes/No**

Victim Age (Approximate if necessary) and Gender: _____

Offender Age (Approximate if necessary) and Gender: _____

Under agreed protocols, would there be circumstances in which you might:

a) approach the 'offender' to ask if they would like to work with the media? **Yes/No**

b) approach the 'victim' to ask if they would be happy to work with the media? **Yes/No**

c) As a practitioner, be available to work with the media? **Yes/No**

Brief description of offence:
Notable issues in this case? _____

_____

_____

_____

Did this case involve contact with both victim and offender? **Yes/No**

Was there a face-to-face meeting involved? **Yes/No**

If yes, did both victim and offender have preparation time with a
Restorative Justice worker? **Yes/No**

If no what was the consultation process for victim and offender? _____

_____

_____

_____

Approximate date case completed _____

(NB: Your definition of completed _____

_____)

Date form completed _____

Other comments: _____

_____

_____

_____

Contacts:

RJ Worker(s) _____

Agency Case Reference (If used): _____

Agency Name: _____

Address: _____

_____

Email: _____ Telephone: _____

Confidentiality Statement:

Nothing will be published without a clear process for checking the anonymity of the parties involved.
Please write down the first names of the victim and the offender so that we can ensure not to use these names.

Please return completed forms to:
RJ Co-ordinator, Mediation UK, Alexander House, Telephone Avenue. Bristol BS1 4BS
THANK YOU FOR YOUR TIME
enquiry@mediationuk.org.uk   Telephone 0117 904 6661   www.mediationuk.org.uk